Have You Discovered Your Assignment with Destiny?

Have You Discovered Your Assignment with Destiny?

Anthony Ugochukwu O. Aliche

DSC. FSM, FPRS, FMRG, FIACC, FNIAM, FABEN

iUniverse, Inc.
Bloomington

Have You Discovered Your Assignment with Destiny?

iUniverse books may be ordered through booksellers or by contacting:

iUniverse
1663 Liberty Drive
Bloomington, IN 47403
www.iuniverse.com
1-800-Authors (1-800-288-4677)

ISBN: 978-1-4759-3664-3 (sc)
ISBN: 978-1-4759-3665-0 (hc)
ISBN: 978-1-4759-3666-7 (ebk)

Library of Congress Control Number: 2012912309

Printed in the United States of America

iUniverse rev. date: 07/17/2012

Truth Is Universal Publishers
28 Okpu-Umuobo Rd.
PO Box 708, Aba
Abia State
Nigeria
Tel: 08037065227, 08059227752, 08064718821
Website: truthisuniversalng.org
E-mail: info@truthisuniversalng.org
truthisuniversalpublishers@yahoo.com

Contents

Dedication

This immortal work, which is from the consummate labyrinth of destiny, is deservingly dedicated to President Goodluck Ebelechukwu Jonathan, whose ascension to the presidency is all about his destiny; to Nelson Mandela, whom I designate as the Christ of South Africa; and to all purpose-driven leaders who discovered their assignment with destiny and used it to uplift humanity.

About
Truth Is Universal Publishers

This diverse, dynamic, and highly inspired organization was founded by Anthony U. Aliche along with several gifted and apostolic scholars. It was established to carry out the important task of providing humanity with great works, including a line of books. These works are gaining universal recognition.

We are compelled and inspired to establish a mind—and purpose-driven universal bank whose activities are centred on *creating a museum of knowledge for the balanced wisdom of posterity.*

Located at Aba in Abia State, Nigeria, with branches in Europe and the United States, Truth is Universal Publishers is a nonsectarian, non-dogmatic organization which operates principally and tactfully in the medium of the universal mind. It imparts honest and strict principles that foster greater awareness of spiritual tenets in the lives of humans.

This institution is highly involved in propagating wisdom and truth, particularly in the areas of religion, health, psychology, science, engineering, technology, philosophy, and spiritualism—stimulating a colloquium of integrated and balanced education.

We also have begun an online study, research, and development programme, Truth is Universal Educational Outreach, with members all over the world. This programme gives people the rare opportunity to explore beyond the boundaries of their present knowledge.

For more information on this organization and its programmes, please write to Truth is Universal Publishers, 28 Okpu-Umuobo Rd., PO Box 708, Aba, Nigeria. You can reach us by telephone at 082-225217, 08037065227, 08059227752, or 08064718821; on our website, Truthisuniversalng.org; or by e-mail at info@truthisuniversalng.org or truthisuniversalpublishers@yahoo.com and on facebook-http://www.facebook.com/TruthIsUniversalPublishers, http://www.facebook.com/profile.php?id=100001817099148.

Global Praise for
Professor Aliche and His Works

"My beloved son Anthony Ugo. O. Aliche follows in the footsteps of my late husband, Dr. Walter Russell, who is widely considered a modern Leonardo Da Vinci."

Dr. Lao Russell, former president,
University of Science and Philosophy, Virginia

"You most certainly are an 'ordained author'! Indeed, you are creating a museum of knowledge for the balanced wisdom of posterity. The key word is *balance*. As we both know, we are living in a most unbalanced world of man/woman thinking and lack of higher consciousness."

Michael Hudak, president,
University of Science and Philosophy, Virginia

"Only an adept writer, and someone of the author's status, could convincingly inject fresh interpretations of existing mathematical and philosophical functions and symbols, as he has done in this book. In doing so, he guides us to the obvious and incontrovertible conclusion that the field of philosophical mathematics is indispensable to the solution of human problems in the past, present, and future. His writings guarantee the continuous relevance, utility, and applicability of the discipline of philosophical mathematics.

Perhaps the most significant of this book's merits is its originality. The author does a minimum of quoting from others. Instead, he generates much of the information, which is amazingly exotic and therefore could have been derived only from the supernatural realm or inspired sources. Not many authors are so gifted!"

Prof. Mkpa Agu Mkpa, former vice-chancellor,
Abia State University, on
The Dynamic Concepts of Philosophical Mathematics by Prof. Aliche

"Your book *What Makes Great Men* is on the top the bestseller list. I have read it entirely, and it is inspiring. Maintain that spirit."

Pastor Praise Michael Daniels, Abuja, Nigeria

"Surely you must be the most published author in Africa! Most important is your continuous effort to awaken and enlighten humanity to the power of loving one another and the gift of loving service to our fellow man or woman! I have looked at your website and feel a greater appreciation for your love of humanity. We both are committed to the unending effort to raise the consciousness of our fellow world citizens to a new way of thinking and acting as we live our lives."

Michael Hudak, president,
University of Science and Philosophy,
Virginia

"Your works aim to restore the dignity of man, and they are destined for global acknowledgement. The fact that it is climbing the bestseller list in Abuja is a sign of the avalanche of global recognition that will follow this selfless and cerebral author of our time. Congratulations, sir, my dear mentor."

Ibe Edede, Port Harcourt, Nigeria

"I am a fan of your series, and I remain grateful to my friend who bought me a copy of your work *Whose Vessel are You*. It dawned on me then that I could be an empty vessel, and I really understood what it means to be a true vessel. I decided that I would be a golden vessel, made for the Master's use.

Bless you, sir. You are a true vessel."

Adimchimnobi Ezinne, Lagos, Nigeria

"Prof. Aliche, you are a genius of the highest order! In all my life as an IT specialist, I have not seen this type of interpretation of information technology and information communication technology. It is a great work."

Eno Etuk, Port Harcourt, Nigeria

"Professor, the northerners in the cabinet of Kastina state government under Gov. Shehu Shema are in love with your articles on metaphysics."

Ovie Ben, editor-in-chief,
The President Afrique Magazine

"I know you are an authority in many different fields of human endeavor, and I encourage and congratulate your dynamic wisdom in exploring the boundless world.

All of us at the world headquarters are grateful to honour and designate you as our new Nigerian chairman and to supervise the metaphysical activities in other African countries."

John J. Williamson, president/founder,
College of Metascientists,
Archer's Court, England

"You are indeed an excellent and brilliant friend whose vast knowledge of nature and its dynamism deserves to be understudied."

Prof. Ralph Onwuka

"Aliche has shown the world that he is a true and perfect breed of the Russellian scientist/philosopher. His achievements, which will be favoured by posterity, must certainly dazzle his contemporaries."

Laara Lindo, former president,
University of Science and Philosophy

"Anthony U. Aliche is an illumined mystic from the East. I respect the comprehensiveness of his ingenuity, particularly his rare gift of considering everybody as one."

Nanik Balani, India

"My esteemed friend Anthony U. O. Aliche is best described as a rare gift to humanity, living a life that appears unequalled in our present, chaotic age. To God be the glory for his esteemed and universal intelligence."

Dr. Singh, India

"After studying *What Is Beyond Truth* on my visit to Nigeria, I discovered that great talent can be found in this humble country, the most populous in Africa. I invite noble souls who appreciate the wisdom of truth to buy this book and analyze it in order to appreciate the fact that nothing is beyond truth."

Prof. Harley Enoch

"Your books are greatly inspiring. After studying *The Mystical Powers of Our Lord's Prayer*, I was personally inspired to honour the wisdom of the Celestial Sanctum. Thank God for your person."

Nick Helen, South Africa

"My great friend is a gifted and rare scholar of our race. I respect and love him particularly for his humility, honesty, and intelligence, and for his accomplished, purpose-driven life."

Sen. Millford Okilo,
former governor of Old Rivers State,
first African president
of the University of Science and Philosophy

"Surely you are the legend of our race!"

Senior staff of the Federal Ministry
of Culture and Tourism, Nigeria

"You are truly a blessing to our nation. I bought your book *Honey Is Health* from Ogbete market, and I am so glad I bought it. I have never thought of honey in this way. God bless you for your knowledge."

Tony Udedike, Enugu State, Nigeria

"You are indeed a 'mobile encyclopedia'!"

Participant at the Garden City Literary Festival,
September 12-17, 2011,
Presidential Hotel, Port Harcourt

"Nnana Aliche, you were born great. Many were not aware of this truth; others knew it but refused to accept it. Your life in the service of humanity will be rewarded not only on earth but eternally. Amen."

Dr. Anthony E. Torty, CEO,
Malic International Services, Ltd.

"You are awarded as a role model and the author of the year as one of the twenty distinguished Nigerians who have, through hard work and excellence, put Nigeria on the world map."

African Child Foundation

A. U. Aliche's Exaltation and Celebration of Wisdom

- ❖ Wisdom is the Omnipotent, Omniscience, Omnipresent, Omni cosmic manifestation of God in practical and symbolic forms
- ❖ It is the consummate and celebrated Alpha and Omega which fathomed and fulcrmed the ingenious design of the universe whose concept has remained a great mystery to the academic and intellectual world
- ❖ It is the absolute power of every thing
- ❖ Wisdom is more than an expert in any field
- ❖ It is beyond the ingenuity of a respected specialist
- ❖ Wisdom is more than a genius
- ❖ It is a rarified force which empowers and puts our destiny to a dynamic function
- ❖ It is the knower and the knowledge of all
- ❖ Wisdom is the Consummate Architect of all ages
- ❖ It authored man and gave him all the necessary powers some of them he does not even know how to make perfect and practical use of for his own enablement and ennoblement
- ❖ Wisdom made the celebrated best of Scientists, Engineers, Technologists, Philosophers, Mystics, Avatars, Geniuses, Inventors and all which have been beneficial to Creation
- ❖ Wisdom is the astrology, the astronomy, and the sea captain of all Ages both present and past
- ❖ It made the forests, the seas, the mountains, the deserts, the waves and what more! It is everything in all things

❖ Wisdom is the Eternal power which decreed **"let there be light"** and there was LIGHT which shows that only in the Absolute Light of wisdom dwells all things both bright and beautiful which shows that wisdom is the super mystery of all ages.

Dedicated to the Consummate Immortality of Illumined Wisdom

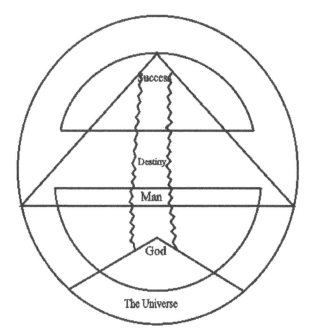

**The Symbol of Destiny as divinely revealed
at the proximity of the author's inspiration.**

Acknowledgement

In writing an acknowledgement to a book that will serve both our modern era and posterity as a means of human enabling, I must begin by recognizing the early use and application of purpose-driven concepts.

First, I need to acknowledge the famous hall of destiny, the highly illumined oriental wizards who continue to be practical teachers to people of all eras: Plato, Pythagoras, Socrates, Emmanuel Kant, Max Miller, Euclid, Albert Einstein, Michael Faraday, Sir Isaac Newton, Sir Isaac Pitman, Dr. Walter Russell, Walt Whitman, Andrew Carnegie, Ralph Waldo Emerson, Lao Russell, Joseph Smith Jr., and other such humans whose lives have become an apostolic foundation of ingenious destiny.

This book cannot accomplish its monumental task without focusing on the life of Christopher Columbus, whose predestined assignment to discover the New World was prophetically revealed in the Book of Isaiah. This great adventure played a noble role in making America discover its own assignment with destiny, whose wisdom is encapsulated in the national motto In God We Trust.

Among the past and modern writers who deserve a place in this monumental hall of fame is William Shakespeare, who has not been equaled within the annals of literature and creative arts, and our contemporary Nobel laureate, Wole Soyinka, who must be seen as the African iroko of literary dynamism. I also wish to acknowledge other apostolic authors like Prof. Chinua Achebe, who wrote the prophetic *Things fall Apart*, and Prof. Vincent Chukwuemeka Ike, destined to be the first chairman of West African Senior School Certificate Examination (WASSCE) when it was separated from Cambridge.

Other important dignitaries who were destined to be placed and remembered in this hall of fame include Bill Clinton, the former president of the United States; Pope John Paul II, who was prophetically destined from the mystical province of the Gnostics; Microsoft founder Bill Gates, who has conquered the world of software technology; and the black Americans whose parents were sold into slavery in the United States, represented in the person of Barack Obama, who was destined to be president of the richest and largest democratic country in the universe.

Other great emperors of destiny who should be mentioned in this titanic list of acknowledgements include Dr. Nyerere Anyim, Sen. Nkechinyere Nwogu, and Lord Quines, who was inspired to give the world an unusual beverage popular among the old and young, and whose destined ingenuity has touched the lives of more than fifty million humans all over the world.

As wisdom is wealth, we must appreciate that the objective use and application of destiny creates wealth. That is why we should acknowledge destined trademarks like PZ, Lever Brothers, International Equitable Association, AP, Glo, MTN, Etisalat, Zain, etc., along with their founders and leaders.

We must also acknowledge the immortal works of Jesus, the central figure of the destined annunciation of Christmas, as well as Buddha, Lao Tse, the Prophet Muhammad, and all who formed the province of the Twelve World Teachers.

At this point, I'd like to thank the whole family of Truth is Universal Publishers, whose purpose-driven destiny is to create a museum of knowledge for the balanced wisdom of posterity. Not only do Ali Farms, Cradle and Concept Consultants, and Queen of Peace Health Services deserve acknowledgement for their impeccable contributions to the growth of human evolution, but their staff members, with Rejoice C. Adiele as a senior task team leader, require an ovation for allowing themselves to be driven by the consuming fire of destiny.

My family also deserves high marks for their practical and spiritual support.

Our admirers and readers from all over the world, and the institutions that contributed to my training, deserve recognition, as well. It will be difficult to mention here all those who should be acknowledged. But with my usual thought-provoking creativity, I hereby acknowledge them all through the greater acknowledgement of the ingenious founder of destiny, who is none other than the Destined Universal One, who has endowed man with irrevocable natural and spiritual gifts. These gifts go to show that from our mother's womb we are destined to be co-creators, key players, co-actors with other destined humans who will use the eternal wisdom of the Creator to promote the course of human evolution. That is why I'll conclude this acknowledgement with an important question: *Have you discovered your assignment with destiny?*

Quotes from the Destined Bank of Anthony Ugochukwu Aliche

The wonders of destiny are seen in its achievements.

Of all the virtues, destiny is the highest.

Man does not know that destiny is the author of knowledge and wisdom.

The discovery of destiny turns a dullard into a genius.

Of all the gifts of Mother Nature, destiny stands tallest. It is supreme.

Ask for your destiny, and you have asked for everything.

Destiny is the original wisdom of the craftsman.

The original meaning of the sun, the moon, and the stars is destiny.

Until you know and learn from destiny, you have not known or learned.

You are never complete until your destiny blesses others.

———————

Your life will be miserable when you waste your destiny.

Waste is the real enemy of destiny.

How wondrous is the womb and destiny of Mother Nature, who did not waste us.

A love for the destiny of Africa is a supreme love for the global family.

Parents, guide your children along the path of their destiny.

Destiny is infectious when you desire to discover your assignment with her.

Human effort alone cannot propel one's destiny; spiritual strength is required.

Destiny has laws, principles, policies, and practices. Your duty is to make people understand those illumined tenets.

What can't we achieve when we bless and blend our efforts with the visionary wisdom of destiny!

Destiny is a holy and revered asset.

Delays are dangerous to people who do not understand that God has a perfect time for everything.

The divine and consummate destiny of Christmas brought the joy of eternal love to humanity.

Ask yourself this eternal question: Who made me, and how and why? Your answers will lead you to the meaning of birth and rebirth.

———

Great minds affirm that destiny is the spiritual current of
God.
That is why the positive use of destiny creates enduring
arts, of which man is a real symbol of divine destiny.

The best of academicians is a student of destiny. Great
arts are the creations of wisdom and destiny.

Destiny gave wisdom to the immortal geniuses.

Destiny acts as the altar and temple of your blessings.

People who know the power of destiny live without
discrimination.

My teacher mandated me to seek my destiny, for in it lies
my well-being.

To celebrate the achievements of your destiny is to
celebrate God.

All the scriptures were written by the light of destiny.

Foreword 1

The subject of destiny has inspired various explanations from diverse schools of thought. While some people believe in and espouse the philosophy of predestination, others believe that man is the architect of his own destiny, while still others do not believe in the concept of destiny at all. Even among those who believe in the concept, there is a lack of consensus about its definition and function. Given the critical nature of the subject, and the need for man to clearly understand destiny and employ that knowledge in his journey from mortality to immortality, the author has done a great job in guiding the reader through that process.

In this detailed presentation on the topic, Professor Anthony Aliche takes the reader through thirty-two chapters, each of which addresses an important segment of the topic. The details of the content of each chapter will not be explained here, as they are succinctly summarized in chapter 32.

As one would expect, the book starts with a lamentation about man's inability to acknowledge and define his destiny. The author makes particular reference to his assignment with his own destiny, his obligation to his environment, and his assignment with the Creator and the entire cosmos. He believes that life lived without discovering one's assignment with destiny is life lived without putting God first, and consequently a life tragically wasted.

The author presents many definitions of *destiny*—some his own, some quoted from authorities in the field—one which presents it as God's consummate authority, which when properly utilized by the beholder, extols him as a co-creator, beholds him as a lover of truth, and inspires him to do things that will help humanity to grow. By implication, therefore, man's destiny should be purpose-driven and applied toward the development of humanity.

It is interesting to consider the author's analyses of the origin, power, and purpose of destiny, as well as his examples of people throughout human history who discovered and effectively used their assignment with destiny to improve the quality of man's life on earth. The effective application of man's assignment with destiny was manifested in some of the greatest achievements in science and technology, literature and the arts, politics and governance, and various other fields of human endeavor.

The author urges readers to move beyond the prevailing spirit of complacency and lethargy and consciously explore their potential, developing and using it to serve God and man. Throughout this book, Professor Aliche extols the benefits of man's dependence on God and the primary role of our Lord Jesus Christ if man is to discover and accomplish his destiny on earth. God-consciousness, belief and trust in the Lord, responsible and responsive living, are indispensable in man's quest to discover and accomplish his assignment with destiny.

This book, therefore, is a call to all humanity to consider the irrevocable role of destiny in human existence. In doing so, it offers answers to the following questions:

- ❑ How pleasant would our world have been if all people discovered and accomplished their assignments with destiny?
- ❑ How terrible would our world have been if no one ever discovered and accomplished his assignment with destiny?
- ❑ Can we therefore infer that the extent to which humankind is happy and comfortable is measured by the extent to which humans have discovered and accomplished their assignment with destiny?

And here's the follow-up question that naturally arises from those above: How can humans learn to appreciate the need to understand the subject of destiny and apply that knowledge productively? Can national educational systems be useful in this regard? It's possible—if we are courageous enough to embrace with open minds, and without suspicion, this all-important but esoteric subject, which is implicit in most world religions when they are examined intelligently. And that is exactly what Professor Anthony Aliche has done in this great work.

We therefore invite all lovers of spiritual development, all earnest seekers of enlightenment, and all who can grapple with fairly sophisticated language to avail themselves of the opportunities that this book offers. We all must learn the indispensable subject of destiny and how we can pursue and accomplish our assignment with it. There appears to be no alternative if we are to live practically and productively.

Mkpa Agu Mkpa

Foreword 2

I have seen people struggle to find a purpose for their life; I have seen people wander through life with no direction and no destination, even people at a later stage in life. They struggle endlessly in stressful jobs they do not like, live in places that do not give them joy, and stay in rancourous relationships that give them more pain than love and passion.

I have also heard and seen people die along with their dreams. I have seen visions and talents wasted, and so many houses in ruins. This happens because of ignorance, because we fail to discover our passion, or because we lack the courage to face our dreams.

Sometimes I ask myself what kills our childish zeal—the enthusiasm you see in growing children who, when asked, "What do you want to be when you grow up?" quickly reply, "A doctor," "A lawyer," or "A pilot." Somehow, children just know and believe that they can be what they want to be. So what happens along the way to stop them from fulfilling their childhood dreams?

Discovering a passion and then nursing that passion to maturity requires boldness and courage. In the case of children, parents and teachers have a duty not to discourage them but to guide them to their destiny. One destiny discovered has a great impact in the world. At the discovery of his destiny, Christopher Columbus gave rise to a new world and a new dimension of human existence on earth. If he had reneged at the call of destiny, if he had refused to follow his dream, what might have happened? What about the

Lander brothers or Mary Slessor, with her passion for missionary work in Africa? Today that destiny discovered has liberated many twins and kept them alive to fulfill their own destinies. It was destiny that made Esther the queen of King Ahasuerus's kingdom; perhaps her destined royalty was for the purpose of liberating her people, the Jews. And the destiny of Christ in Christmas is the only reason we live today.

How about your own destiny? Have you discovered your assignment with destiny? Do you realize that many people's lives may be hanging on your destiny?

In this great work, Professor Aliche opens our eyes to the fact that a great many lives could make a quantum leap, if only we took a time-out and tuned in to God and nature to discover and make manifest our destiny. While he emphasizes that there are challenges attached to this task, he also reassures us that within those challenges lie catalysts to our success.

It is important to note that it required someone like Professor Aliche—someone who has discovered his own assignment with destiny—to bless this generation, and generations to come, with a book like this one. I therefore encourage all who come across this work to tune in to his inspiration and let the destined grace in this work bring about the manifestation of their own destiny for the betterment of the universal family.

It is my deepest prayer that this work will give strength to those who are about to give up, encourage those who are at the verge of collapse, and reassure them that deep within those thorns could be their destinies, lying fallow. Thus let us arise, break the fallow ground, and rejoice in the victory of discovering our destined ingenuity.

I therefore recommend this work to all who yearn to be a help to our generation. We must not leave this planet without making a positive impact on it. Then, and only then, shall posterity call us blessed.

Thank you for allowing yourself to be used by the great hands of destiny, Professor Anthony Ugochukwu Aliche. We are encouraged and ennobled by the vastness of your ingenious, creative destiny.

Rejoice C. Adiele
Truth is Universal Publishers

Watch Your Thoughts

**Watch your thoughts, for they soon become your words.
Watch your words, for they become your actions.
Watch your actions, for they become your habits.
Watch your habits, for they become your character.
Watch your character, for it becomes your destiny.**

It is here that out-of-the-box thinking, thought creation, and transference take effect.

The subject that we will explain decisively and then dissect philosophically falls naturally within the areas of psychology, philosophy, religion, and meta-psychology. *Objective thinking gives us absolute power based on balanced, technical reasoning.*

"As a man thinketh, in his heart so he becomes." This biblical verse helps explain why so many people today are poor, wretched, and unable to align with their assignment with destiny—it's because of the way they think. How we think determines our character, our destination, our level of personal enrichment, our human connectivity and creativity, and our relationship with the spiritual world.

It's important to understand that thought has a natural origin, and that someone who does not think positively goes against the natural law of consummate creativity. This law is the driving force behind all the great minds of all ages: the great thinkers, achievers, philosophers, inventors, scientists, engineers, industrialists, and entrepreneurs.

Our failure to answer this natural law has compounded the many challenges of our contemporary era. I've received requests from students all over the world asking me to produce a work that will help man understand that it's not possible to conquer poverty and mediocrity and discover our global destiny without right thinking, synchronized with right action.

Many people argue that thinking is the occupation of the brain, while others believe that it also is a function of the spirit. Those who believe that thinking is the occupation of the brain alone are uninformed. That is why it must be established with scientific statements that thinking is more a spiritual act than a mental one. Note that every human invention and craft began with natural inspiration. In that respect, what and when you think are very important in shaping your destiny, for soon you will voice your thoughts, and then—consciously or not—you will act on those words. Before you know it, these actions will metamorphose into habits, and if these habits are not controlled, they will be reflected in your character. Behold your destiny, shaped and accepted by you!

Consider this story:

A boy named Jack was told by a fortune-teller that he would be a king. He had no royal lineage—not a single connection to royalty. But although he was poor and wretched, Jack instantly tapped into this inner greatness. He wore the cheapest of clothes, but he tried to add a unique touch that set him apart from other children, like a flower or anything that made him feel special and distinct. His friends laughed at him, knowing full well that he had no link to royalty, but Jack was not perturbed. He began walking majestically and took a lot of pleasure in watching the comportment of kings and queens, princes and princesses. He learned to speak like a king, with a commanding presence; he soon began actually acting a king. He took delight in giving the few coins he had to those he felt were in greater need than he was—hoping to give others the chance to live like a king, too. "Keep the balance," Jack would always say.

Before long, Jack's mates started imitating him—trying to do what he did and speak as he spoke. More people wanted to be his friend, because when they went out together, Jack was given special treatment due to the way he carried himself. Jack soon had many followers and listeners, and in no time he was made the head boy in school, the school authorities having recognized his leadership qualities. From then on, Jack continued to be a leader wherever he found himself, and eventually his royal character formed his destiny—he was a king, after all.

Think it, speak it, act it, live it . . . and behold your destiny!

To think, therefore, is to answer the call of nature, putting the mind to work in order to liberate the brain from dormancy. When we think, we electrify our mind, which in turn ignites the spirit, propelling us to work, to act, to reason, to appreciate, and to understand. In metaphysical psychology, for example, thinking goes with thought transference; the byproduct of thinking is what thought transference uses to carry out its meta-psychological and psychic assignments.

Introduction

A look at the timeline of science, showing the evolution of its mechanisms, systems, and concepts, reveals that many people don't understand what is in a name, while others do not recognize their assignments with destiny. This implies that most times, the name you call yourself is what others will accept. If you think good of yourself and call yourself such, people may not have option than to follow suit. In fact, most people have carelessly ignored their God-given ingenuity hence, allowing mediocrity to define their character.

Only God-inspired wisdom, translated into the material through creative writing, can become a bestseller like *Have You Discovered Your Assignment with Destiny?* This thought-provoking book, timeless and enlightening, will stir a spiritual reawakening with its inherent genius. It will lead us to the honest pathway that we were nobly created to follow in God's image.

This book was written with the encouragement of Rejoice C. Adiele and her gracious co-workers. After helping develop the vision for this book, they established through research and discussion that no writer has ever before delved into the subject in this format, revealing the sacrosanct ingenuity of destiny.

The word *sacrosanct* here is the verbal actualization of the concept of destiny, which falls within the creative realm of psychology, astronomy, religion, and mysticism. People recognize this connection when they say, "I am a destined child," "My success is my destiny,"

"To God be the glory for my destiny," "Destiny is unchangeable," or "Destiny can be delayed but not stopped." Destiny, in other words, is God's inherent star, God's inherent gift, God's inherent wisdom. It elevates us all, particularly those who strive to discover the genius within that destiny.

Destiny has many definitions, which we can see by looking at the many ways people have succeeded—through creative inventions, intellectual prowess, industrial engineering, academic achievement, political skill, or philosophical inspiration. But one thing is common among them: God is always the fulcrum, the author of our destiny. Manly Palmer Hall describes this dynamically in his book *America's Assignment with Destiny,* which reveals him as a tutor, revealer of truths, and philosopher, as well as a life guide and comprehensive educator.

When we consider destiny in this respect, the question, Have you discovered your assignment with destiny? can be rephrased as, Have you discovered your reality with the Creator—the purpose for which you were created?

In some schools of thought, destiny is defined by seeking astrological insight into our spiritual life. This perspective explains why it is possible for a pauper to become a king, a king to become a president, a president to become a nation builder, and a nation builder to become a continental governor. But the science of destiny can be appreciated only when we focus on God, who can reveal the reason behind our individual destinies. This is the story behind the achievement of the Twelve World Teachers, the great philosophers, the illumined musicians, and the greatest geniuses and mystics the world has ever had.

Your assignment with destiny, when you discover it, will take you to the pinnacle of success. It will make you a universal force, bringing you to the corridors of infinite power with its multifarious blessings and graces.

It was destiny that ignited Michael Faraday to give a name—electricity—to an invisible current that he was not able to comprehend, a force that cannot be analyzed in terms of dimension or mathematics alone.

Looking back to the ingenious creations of the oriental apostolate, we discover that the subject of destiny was the key factor driving their immeasurable inventions and contributions to the world of knowledge.

It is important to explain that during the creation of this book, inspiration was simply using the honest writer as a vessel, who, when he discovered the poetic rhythm of this work, exclaimed, "Oh God of our forefathers, I hand over myself to thee so that you can lead me to discover my assignment with destiny."

His peers retorted, "A great and glorious person is one who has been able to discover his assignment. That is why the organist's inspired orchestra, those who helped this work evolve, all concurred in its theme: that to know, discover, appreciate, and utilize your purpose-driven assignment with destiny is the greatest thing that can happen to you during your earthly life."

The author of this book wholly believes that our assignment with destiny, when properly discovered and utilized, is the only force capable of creating a well of genius that will serve us into posterity, and that those who do not understand their assignment with destiny fail to apply God's genius to positive action. The fortunate ones who have discovered their assignment with destiny are always singing, "We must hail the glory of the Creator, for his blessings and gifts endureth forever."

How dignified is the power of destiny.

Shakespeare defined his literary prowess in the might of destiny, while A. U. Aliche defined his ingenious creativity in the monumental wisdom of destiny.

The Philosophy of This Book

This book objectively and dynamically explores the purpose and concept of destiny. It aims to facilitate man's development; his awareness of truthful principles; and his understanding of why destiny is divine, spiritual, and mystical, and especially why it is the only institution capable of helping us appreciate the spiritual nature of things.

Philosophy is known as the mother of science, with different segmental rubrics aimed at achieving the concept of purity and perfection. Destiny is involved in the objective use of purpose-driven philosophical principles, applied with consummate and perfect wisdom.

It is sad to observe that man, who was supremely designed by the Creator, has been unable to know his assignment with destiny, which includes the following:

- his natural assignment with himself
- his divine obligation to his environment
- his destined assignment with the Creator
- his mandate to carefully and objectively study nature, which adheres strictly to the immortal laws of destiny
- his assignment to explore the destiny of the cosmos, where we fall between the two segmental rubrics of ingeniously destined creativity.

The purpose of this work is to reawaken humans who are still dormant in the objective conception of life's reality.

―――――

When we look at what constitutes balanced knowledge and creative wisdom, it's clear that the humans we most respect and immortalize are those who were able to utilize their assignments with destiny, exemplified by the ennobled souls of the Twelve World Teachers.

In our contemporary era, the evolving man still has a lot to do, investigate, and experiment with. Discovering our assignment with destiny will enlighten us and cause a spiritual awakening, helping us appreciate that we are naturally out of alignment with the supernatural forces of destiny, with the supernatural force of the Creator.

It is important to demystify the sacredness of destiny so others can use it to empower themselves, their families, and their country.

Michael Faraday started early enough in his life to discover his assignment with destiny: what we celebrate today as the field of electromagnetism.

Pythagoras, in his own era, discovered his assignment with destiny as an immortal oracle of mathematics.

William Shakespeare was labeled the oracle of literary wisdom because he discovered his assignment with destiny.

Many people have contributed immeasurably to the development of the universe by using their destiny to the glory of the Creator. That is why this work, with its lavish structure and noble concepts, centres around one question: Have you discovered your assignment with destiny?

It is important to explain that the fact that one is a president of a country, and even the bishop or the pastor of a church, does not necessarily mean that he has discovered his assignment with destiny. Most respected people—academicians and professors, for example—are not in their exalted positions, because they have discovered their assignments with destiny. A president's contributions and creations do not last beyond the period of time he is in office.

But humans who have discovered their destiny have found a divine ministry; they are always working to reawaken humanity, creating immortal works which will benefit man into posterity.

It is a pity that we have not fully explored why certain people are considered great. Why do we celebrate the lives of people like Jesus Christ, Moses, Daniel, David, Joseph, Joshua, Buddha, Muhammad, Plato, and Socrates? Why do we celebrate the immeasurable contributions of the apostles and disciples of the past who carried out the blessing and assignment of consummate divinity? Those contributions—their supreme quest for the grail—have remained the hope of the past, present, and future.

Some people might be baffled by this work, this new version of the supreme message of the gospel truth and eternal wisdom. But earthly life that is not lived in accordance with destiny is vanity upon vanity. This is why when Solomon discovered his assignment with destiny, he quickly enrolled as a student of the celestial institution where he was taught through the ingenuity of destined wisdom. After graduation he courageously lamented that his past life had been lived for material glory—vanity upon vanity.

When the key of destiny was bestowed upon me by the supreme Creator, inspiration opened my eyes. The Holy Spirit helped me understand that this book, which came in the form of a question, would lift up human souls, helping others appreciate that a life lived without discovering one's assignment with destiny is life lived without putting God first, without being in perfect union with truth. *Have You Discovered Your Assignment with Destiny?* will answer the age-old question, Man, how do you stand before your Creator? For "in vain we build the city if we do not first build the man."

Have You Discovered Your Assignment with Destiny? brings you in close touch with the inherent genius that is free to all who commit to the Creator. His relationship to us is always purpose-driven, helping us discover our destiny. That's a process which, when well utilized, places us at the heart of the Holy Spirit, who indeed is the river of the living waters.

IMAGINE HOW BEAUTIFUL THE
WORLD WOULD BE IF WE ALL
DISCOVERED THE REASON AND
PURPOSE FOR WHICH WE LIVE

What Can be Accepted as the Original Wisdom of this Book?

Authors all over the world write without revealing the original wisdom that serves as the fulcrum of this book. That's because such authors do not write from the standpoint of the purpose-driven principle of destiny. Many of them are not led by the inspiration that makes any creative work an immortal asset with a timeless concept.

The title of this work—*Have You Discovered Your Assignment with Destiny?*—requires that we explore the wisdom, philosophy, and purpose of the book, and especially its spiritual ontology. By explaining the human appetite for discovery and the quality of destiny, the book certainly covers new ground within the annals of human psychology. This is so because destiny is a great asset, and its manifestation exalts the person who explores it.

This book, inspired by original wisdom, is aimed at making man ask himself whether he has discovered his own assignment with destiny. In order to do so, the book encourages him to answer the following questions:

- ❖ Do I have the desire to discover my destiny?
- ❖ Can destiny be copied, or is it original in every man?
- ❖ What are the powers and functions of destiny?
- ❖ How does the objective application of our destiny make a path for us?

- ❖ Why is destiny defined as journeying in the light of truth?
- ❖ Can seeking one's destiny be defined as a profession?
- ❖ Can destiny be utilized as a source of enlightenment?
- ❖ How is destiny tied to the objective rhythm of nature?
- ❖ What factors enhance the objective and spiritual function of destiny?
- ❖ Why are 99 percent of humans living their life without having discovered their assignment with destiny?
- ❖ How can we create awareness to enlighten people and motivate them to start discovering their destiny in accordance with God's purpose?
- ❖ Why is destiny defined as a living and monumental symbol of man's ingenuity?
- ❖ What can we do to fall in line with the driving spiritual force of destiny?
- ❖ Why did Solomon decide with spiritual courage to discover his destiny?
- ❖ Why did Solomon's enlightenment make him the wisest man since the dawn of consciousness?
- ❖ Should we take a spiritual or physical approach to discovering our destiny?
- ❖ How does discovering our destiny impact our educational policy and system?
- ❖ What is the role of religion, with its multifarious dogmas, in ensuring that our destiny is practically realized?

The answers to these questions form the foundation that determines the nature, wisdom, power, force, concept, and concerns of destiny.

At all levels of human and spiritual endeavor, wisdom is destined to be driven by the authoritative ingenuity of nature. Even human symbols can be considered an aggregate of ingenious creative destiny. When destiny is discovered along with its monumental assignment, it is naturally powerful, creative, purposeful, constant, wonderful, anointing, inspiring, and desiring. Its objective use spiritually inspires us to become ministers of truth and love, ministers of the holy current that is driven, led by the Holy Spirit.

This is why this book seeks to impact, reveal, explain, and buttress our discovery of our assignment with destiny and help us have absolute control of that destiny.

The American assignment with destiny is revealed in its national motto, In God We Trust. This motto shows the United States as a nation of the New World, the nation known all over the universe as a symbol of world power through the use and application of creative destiny.

These introductory pages show the philosophy of this book, based on purposeful wisdom and an anointing vision, and they expose the ontology of this work. May the millions who come across this book and read its introduction accept it as consummate wisdom, including the recital of those words, *In God We Trust*.

Inspired by wisdom, the author of this book concludes with the glorious revelation that man, destiny, and God are partners, prophets, and teachers. That is why in order to define the wisdom of this book, we must always reveal a truth in perfect and practical agreement with the title of the book. *Have You Discovered Your Assignment with Destiny?* will serve our contemporary era and posterity as an encyclopedia of wisdom and a complement to balanced, objective knowledge. Just as wisdom is wealth, destiny, when objectively used, creates enduring wealth through the absolute fulfillment of God's ingenious assignment. When we desire to discover our assignment with destiny, we experience peace and love because our destiny paves the way to wisdom in practice and manifested in our cooperation with God and our inspiration by the Holy Spirit. We also appreciate the destined power of Jesus Christ, whom some of us have never before known. That is the only way we can live a purpose-driven life.

What is the purpose of this book, with its ingenious ontology?

To understand the purpose of this book, with its ingenious ontology, it must be appreciated that destiny is the way of truth and success, exalting the one who has discovered his assignment with it. That is why this work serves to reveal man's assignment with destiny; destiny's assignment with creation; and, in turn, creation's assignment with destiny. It is here that the book's ingenious ontology comes into play as a divine virtue with eternal values.

Sadly, many people do not understand the meaning of destiny or its purpose and wisdom. They are still in the dark ages of evolution; they have yet to know the segmental rubrics which form and propel various destinies.

When we reflect on the achievements of the great souls whom we respect and regard as immortals, we can see that their assignments with destiny were manifested in objective lives. This is why we must strive honestly to discover our own assignment with destiny, so that we can be similarly fulfilled.

Given this truth, the purpose and ontology of this work, with its ingenious rhythm, is to explain the following:

❑ If you are a teacher, your teaching methods and techniques must be purpose-driven, applying the divine virtues that extol the clear ingenuity of destiny.

❑ If you are a farmer, your farming mechanisms and methods must be synchronized with the directives and objectives of destiny.

❑ If you are a housewife, you must appreciate the values of destiny and the virtues of womanhood. Your instincts and thoughts must motivate you to be a constant example of what a prayerful, spiritually strong wife should be. Only destiny can empower a woman to know that she is both a pillar of the family and a help to her husband. The well-known adage that "behind every great man there is a great woman" only reiterates the validity of destiny in the family structure. This is why for a housewife to live a fulfilled life, she must appreciate with spiritual recognition her assignment with destiny.

❑ If you are an ordained prophet from God, your prophecy must be aligned with the light and voice of divine destiny. This is why great prophets and seers like Elijah, Elisha, Amos, Malachi, and Isaiah were highly extolled, ennobled, exalted, and remembered for their prophetic and loving deeds.

❑ If you are a leader of people, your leadership and service cannot be appreciated if you are not aligned with destiny or if you have not been assigned to lead—that is, if you are not divinely driven to be a true servant of the people. This is why leadership requires many spiritual values, the most important of which are humility, simplicity, honesty, and integrity, as well as being God-fearing and God-loving.

❑ A gifted author cannot write perfectly, and his writings cannot affect and inspire others, if he does not submit to the rhythm and inspiration of the controlling powers of destiny. That's because destiny *is* the author. It is the force and wisdom that direct the author's activities so his works are not ephemeral or simply exercises in intellectual prowess. This is why great authors like Walter Russell, Manly Palmer Hall, William Shakespeare, Herbert Spencer, and Ralph Waldo Emerson are ever immortalized within the annals of inspired creativity.

❑ If you are a philosopher, an engineer, a technologist, or an industrialist, your endeavours cannot see the light of the day if they are not objective manifestations of the thematic ingenuity of destiny. A lot of people who are called "destined children" are those who have lifted themselves up from mediocrity to greatness through ingenuity.

❑ If you are a statesman, your people will continue to suffer as a result of obnoxious laws simply because statesmanship is not your destiny. This is the common problem of our contemporary civilization.

A look at the immortal contributions of Sir Nelson Mandela, Buddha, Mahatma Gandhi, and John F. Kennedy, as well as the life and times of great mystics and the Twelve World Teachers, reveals that destiny serves to glorify the Creator. To fulfill one's destiny is to use the powers and forces of the Creator—becoming, in a sense, a co-creator. Therefore a destined roadside mechanic, a destined carpenter, even a destined nanny is as important as a statesman—they all fulfill God's plan.

This work and its ontology aim to reveal that all of us are destined, but the job of putting destiny into action lies and lives within us. The star of destiny is effectively put into action when we recognize it as the inherent genius that, when properly and objectively utilized, makes a way for us.

In his book *You Can Control Your Destiny*, Mike Omoleye reminds us that the Holy Bible says that God created the world out of nothing, but He fashioned man in His own image. "Many are born to mould their worlds out of nothingness," he writes. "To such people, young or old, who recognize their bondage, I present this book."

In his introduction to that book, Omoleye says many renowned world leaders, past and present, were known to have studied the forces of destiny, subjugating them and then using them for the benefit of mankind. Omoleye notes that while no condition is permanent, destiny can never be changed. He concludes that destiny can be understood at the individual and cosmic levels as the power that is supposed to control events.

A look at this great book reveals that the question driving it is in balanced harmony with the original purpose of the work, with its ingenious ontology. This is a work to examine if you have discovered your assignment with destiny. It comes at a time when the human race is stagnating and even degenerating. That's why the purpose of this work is to reorder things, to reawaken all humans to appreciate that no man is created mediocre; every man is born great, noble, and intelligent, with many destined virtues and qualities. But to put them into effective action remains our mission, because heaven helps those who help themselves. That adage serves as an eloquent testimony to the fact that the heights attained by great men were not the result of sudden flight. We must seek every opportunity, knock on every door, and ask every question to attract the power of heaven, which is the way of practical destiny in action, reaction, rhythm, and enrichment. David sums up the practical path to destiny when he wrote, "Blessed are those who walketh not in the counsel of the wicked." This is the truth with which we can harness the purpose and ontology of our destiny.

"All of us are destined, but the job of putting destiny into action lies and lives within us. The star of destiny is effectively put into action when we recognize it as the inherent genius that, when properly and objectively utilized, makes a way for us."
Anthony Ugochukwu Aliche

Chapter 1

What is destiny?

Since the dawn of consciousness, the subject of destiny—its importance, origin, and power, and the illumined wisdom it contains—has remained a critical and controversial issue which even the best academicians and experts in various fields have not been able to address. From mortality to immortality, man has not been able to discern whether his life is driven by destiny. This is why just a few of the humans who have come into this world have been able to realize their assignments with destiny.

These people are defined and honoured as the Twelve World Teachers; they fall into different categories including cosmic messengers, super mystics, metaphysicists, illumined philosophers, innovators, and inventors. This is why I accepted the task of writing on this serious topic; it was a monumental assignment from the Infinite bank of Mother Destiny.

As commonly understood by millions of humans all over the world, destiny is God in action, when man decides as a vessel of destiny to comply with the ingenious directives of the Creator. The dynamic function of destiny defies explanation; it is beyond ordinary expression. Since the dawn of consciousness, humans have not been able to understand that all our actions—particularly those that help develop the global family—are planned, driven, conceived, and developed by destiny.

Destiny can be defined as nature's greatest and most complex concept, involving the use and application of psychological, spiritual, and meta-transcendental factors. Life is destiny-driven; hence, when our activities are planned under the canopy of destiny, we discover that our lives involve little or no struggle—because destiny is a power and a wisdom mightier than any human engineering.

In this respect, when our life is ordered and governed by destiny, we discover that we naturally become co-creators, authorities in our field even if we have little academic training. Case studies of this are the lives of Jesus Christ, the Prophet Muhammad, Lao-Tse, or Akhenaton. Destiny made Plato develop a metaphysical community that has not been equaled since the dawn of consciousness.

As I write on the subject of destiny, consider these important questions:

- Have you discovered your assignment with destiny?
- Do you know that you are an image of destiny?
- Are you aware that destiny does not work with ego, discrimination, and self-centredness?
- Are you aware that the entire universe, which is a canopy of divine grace, is the province of enlightened destiny?
- Are you aware that "I can try" is a maxim developed and put into practice from the ingenious bank of destiny?
- Do you know that every objective author borrows his words from the consummate pen of destiny?
- Do you know that our lifestyle is determined by creations of destiny that we have not known or put into practice?

A look at these questions makes us understand that destiny is real, it is practical, and it is beyond words and thoughts. This is why it is naturally devoid of all acts and concepts of negativity and speculation.

It is unfortunate that people do not realize that as we have a dual mental system, destiny functions on both the spiritual and physical levels. For example, the application of physical destiny makes people excel in material creativity—in research and inventions, technology, engineering, and science. But spiritual destiny develops our innermost being to think of things divine—to show love, to be our brother's keeper, and to understand that life is a pilgrimage, involving things that tally with the Ten Commandments.

In this respect, we can now appreciate that the dynamic and technological achievements of Michael Faraday, Sir Isaac Newton, Galileo, Albert Einstein, Thomas Edison, and Dr. Walter Russell were manifestations of material destiny, while the victory of Jesus Christ, the achievements of Plato, the mission of Lao-Tse, and the teachings of the Prophet Muhammad were manifestations of spiritual destiny.

It is the mission of this chapter to invite researchers, academicians, and other experts in various fields of human endeavor to investigate what destiny is all about, to appreciate its origin, and to include it in the curriculum of universities around the world. This will help students understand where they belong and appreciate what they are meant to do, because when a student is taught to appreciate his destiny, he will certainly become a great scholar and a genius.

This book is intended to invoke deep and positive thinking, positive action, and positive creativity. The subject of destiny might seem controversial, but it's a great topic which challenges everyone to recognize that we can do nothing when our life and destiny is in slumber. This is why the definition of destiny is best understood by those who appreciate that evolution and civilization are the modest and dynamic outcome of human growth and development.

What is destiny? The question asks us to understand that genius is inherent within us, while mediocrity is self-inflicted. The choice between the two rests with our individual desire. This is why the mandate of this book is to enlighten people, motivating them to work on and cooperate with their assignment with destiny, without which all endeavours become vanity upon vanity. Destiny, in this context, is defined as the living and monumental wisdom of all ages.

_____

A lot of people do not understand the real meaning and purpose of destiny. This is why they have lived their lives without contributing anything meaningful to their generation.

According to the Oxford English Dictionary (OED), *destiny* is defined in the following way:

> What happens to somebody or what will happen to them in the future, especially things that they cannot change or avoid.

When the OED was originally published more than four hundred years ago, this was an accepted definition. But this book will reveal that the original definition is no longer valid.

Webster's defines *destiny* in a bit more detail:

- ❏ State or condition appointed or predetermined; ultimate fate; doom; lot; fortune; destination; destiny as men are solicitous to know their future destiny.
- ❏ Invisible necessity, fate, a necessity or fixed order of things established, as by a divine decree, or by an indissoluble connection of causes and effects.

In *You Can Control Your Destiny*, Mike Omoleye defines *destiny* as

> the channel through which each person realizes the daily experiences of life.

He goes on further to say that an individual's destiny refers to the action of man's will or that freedom of action granted to him by nature to shape his life according to his own desire.

A look at these definitions from different perspectives reveals that none of these authorities was able to capture an impeccable definition of destiny. The author of this book, from the ingenuity of his inspired wisdom that he has adopted as a business necessity and revealer, is empowered and authorized to define destiny as follows:

- ❑ Destiny is God's supreme gift or light or favour or power or providence, which is naturally and spiritually irrevocable.
- ❑ Destiny is God's consummate authority which, when properly utilized by the beholder, extols him as a co-creator, reveals him as a lover of truth, and inspires him to do things that will help humanity grow.
- ❑ Destiny is the spiritual current which, when properly utilized, ennobles one to serve the Creator according to the absolute grace which was bestowed upon him.
- ❑ Destiny is the anatomy and foundation of any great success. This is why its recognition and application will serve humanity while extolling the person beyond his era and above his age and educational level. This is why destiny is defined as God when employed in objective and creative action.

A case study of destiny is found in the story of Solomon, the world's wisest man. He began as a mediocre man with vast material wealth, but later he developed great wisdom through the use and application of destiny.

We can be so many things at a time without realizing our assignment with destiny, without beholding our destiny, without knowing the purpose for which we were created. This is why the ancient thinkers were applauded for their objective use of destiny.

In this respect, destiny can be defined as the science and employment of God's gift for effective service of the universal family. This is why all those who serve honestly are highly ennobled, blessed, enriched, and immortalized—because the pinnacle of destiny is anchored in immortality.

Solomon defined destiny as "God and man in action," while I define destiny as God, man, nature, the Holy Spirit, and Jesus Christ in effective cooperation and noble occupation.

A look at the mysteries and wonders of destiny reveals that all of us are blessed and enriched, but our problems lie in not adhering to the rules and regulations that will help us tap into and utilize our destiny for the betterment of all.

I think of destiny as a wonderful housewife who unconditionally loves her husband. He is the head of the family, his wife is the neck, and the two work together for the benefit of the family, to the wonder and envy of their friends and neighbours.

In this respect, destiny with its objective utilization is the foundation of creation; it has served man as the beginning and culmination of his faith and his mission. The following chapter will reveal the do's and don'ts of destiny, and it will reveal why some people are better off than others financially or spiritually.

History is full of celebrations of great successes, and these celebrations can inspire all of us to learn and work toward our destiny. When this book states that genius is inherent in every man, while mediocrity is self-inflicted, it serves to emphasize that the choice to be destined lies within us, the reason to succeed lies within us, and to strive for success is our mandate. The statement that destiny is a supreme vessel that drives all ingenious creativity is not an angry statement or a mockery of truth. Instead, it is a simple acknowledgment that no human can succeed in life without understanding why he was created, the purpose of creation, the meaning of service, and the wonders and mysteries of God. This is why, in attesting for the water of destiny, which flows directly from the fountain of divinity, I hereby confirm with authoritative wisdom and ingenuity that the principle that determines the definition of destiny lies in, with, and for man.

Destiny is best defined as man in action when the Creator is in purpose-driven motion—man in agreement with the Creator when he submits himself wholly to the controlling power of the Holy Spirit. This is why destiny can be thought of as an eternal and supreme current, right from the foundation of universal creativity.

For the record, destiny is both created by God and creative. It is enduring and empowering. All these qualities make God what He is. Man, too, deserves to cooperate with the owner of destiny, for there is no other way he can realize his spiritual mandate without steadily beholding himself in the mirror of the Creator. Destiny, therefore, is God in action when man is in effective cooperation with his Creator. That is why this book begins with the question, Have you discovered your assignment with destiny?

Think . . .

"Destiny is the spiritual current which, when properly utilized, ennobles one to serve the Creator according to the absolute destiny which was bestowed upon him."
Anthony U. Aliche

"Every people should be the originators of their own designs, the projector of their own schemes, and creators of the events that lead to their destiny—the consummation of their desires."
Martin Robison Delany

"Discover your passion; find out that which makes you happy. Work on it, groom it, and follow that direction. In that lies your destiny."
Rejoice Adiele

Chapter 2

The origin of destiny hereby revealed and examined with the use and application of inspiration, which maintains a spiritual and business purpose with destiny

Our concept of creation has come of age. The science of evolution has revealed that everything has an origin, every origin has perfect and immortal roots, and every root is natural, not magical. Even phenomena that have been defined as magic are materially created. Nature has revealed that she follows an order, that she has a leader.

Nature also has shown that without the power of that leader, she cannot function. As our civilization evolves, one of our greatest scientific challenges is to better understand—and to appreciate on a deeper spiritual level—the origins of natural life.

Like any other thing in life, destiny is created out of an ingenious dominant gift from the supernatural intelligent being—created, in fact, from the monumental rhythm of supernatural intelligence.

It is important to note that the origin of all things is perfectly and absolutely unique, a direct product of the Creator. This is why the universe depends on the Universal One: destiny depends on its supreme origination. It is here that the science and gift of destiny intersect, and the Creator becomes the consummate Monad.

———————

Many people do not understand that destiny is our supernatural gift, part of our inherent nature. It is the ultimate ingenuity that determines what we are going to be, whether we will succeed, when our success will manifest itself, and the power and purpose of its manifestation. Destiny is the supreme answer to the question, What makes great men?

Evolution is no longer understood strictly in terms of religious teachings, theological dogmas, and cultural traditions. The time has come when man and science should acknowledge the Creator's role in evolution so that we will understand what makes Him the consummate super Monad.

The biblical story of creation reveals that destiny has its supreme origin in the abundant ingenuity of the Creator. Its origin is as old as the Creator's celestial statement "Come let us make man in our image."

Therefore our success, our position in life, our well-being—all that makes us a living and cardinal image of God—is spiritual. We are an embodiment of our destiny as anointed by the Creator.

Science was able to separate the Creator from His creations simply because it never made any efforts to seek Him, to seek the purpose and destiny of science, to seek the ingenuity of spirituality and the Super-Genius Monad.

But our life cannot be complete if our destiny is not aligned with our creations, our actions, our reactions, our well-being, and our service to humanity.

The destiny of Jesus Christ, the light of the destined world, is a big lesson for all of us, proving that destiny is strong. In fact, the power of destiny is more lasting and creative than the power of talent.

Destiny is the greatest of God's gifts, which are irrevocable. When harnessed and used well, it makes you a lord over so many other ingenious creations. Talent, on the other hand, is manifested in a single product, an iota of the monumental works of destiny.

Many people have discovered their talents and then used them to create material empires for their own benefit and that of their families. But any man who discovers his assignment with destiny creates original wealth and abundant services for the welfare of the world. This is what we see in the lives of the Twelve World Teachers, great co-creators who used their destiny in service to humanity, in service to God, and in exaltation of themselves. This book encourages you to emulate those teachers by accepting the following spiritual advice:

- ❑ When praying, always ask the Creator to help you to discover your assignment with destiny, not just your talents.
- ❑ Keep in mind that the power of destiny is limitless, revealing our spiritual connectivity with the Infinite Trinity.
- ❑ Man and destiny share the same divine origin. That is why destiny is more supreme than talent. Destiny is an anointing from the spiritual love bank of the Creator.
- ❑ Destiny's living presence in us makes us more active, more creative, more functional, and more dynamic, with pragmatic ideas and concepts. When one discovers his assignment with destiny, he is living in heaven on earth.
- ❑ The power of destiny is the power of love, light, life, truth, and enabling. Since the dawn of consciousness, only a few humans have discovered their assignment with destiny, and only a few countries have been able to discover their assignment with destiny.

So the question, then, is "Are you different from these humans who have discovered their assignment with destiny?"

We cannot discover our assignment with destiny without appreciating the source of our origin, the perfect Creator of all things beautiful and bright. It is the intention of the Creator that all his creations discover their assignment with destiny, the only force that will align us with His creative ingenuity. Therefore this chapter, aside from defining and recognizing the origin of destiny, also seeks designation as an inspired instruction on the works and creations of destiny. This is why it honestly implores all people to discover their assignment with destiny.

Our mandate to make this discovery ennobles us to liberate our destiny, which creates room for our immortality. Simply put, when you realize your destiny, you cannot *die*. You can use destiny to beatify and beautify earthly life. It is a powerful gift, especially when combined with wisdom and talent. Destiny is the only authority that enables us to embody God's will—a dynamic relationship explained in the following passage:

> Blessed are those who are able to discover their assignment with destiny, and to use it perfectly and objectively, for such humans are called the chosen light of God's ingenious creation. They are the perfect way, the truth through which God manifests Himself, His chosen vessels that cooperate with Him as His co-creators.

This is why all human life is purpose-driven, and we all are given the objective assignment of discovering our destiny.

Think . . .

*"Any man who discovers his assignment with destiny creates
original wealth and abundant services for the welfare of
the world."*
Anthony U. Aliche

"It is in your moments of decision that your destiny is shaped."
Anthony Robbins

Chapter 3

What is the power of destiny?

A lot of people, due either to ignorance or to the ephemeral appetites of the ego, are naturally locked out of the corridors of the power of destiny.

Destiny has an immortal power that is blended with consummate and endless wisdom. This is why the power of destiny is creative, enduring and in absolute union with the Creator. The power of destiny is beyond words and thoughts.

A look at the dynamic functions of nature reveals that it uses the objective power of destiny. This is why everything about nature is thematically driven, always dependent upon the law of balanced interchange.

The power of destiny is stronger than any material or economic limitations. Because of that power, the ennobled souls who were able to discover their assignment with destiny have always implored us to seek, knock, ask, learn how to serve, and lift others up. For these are the dominant factors that, working together, determine how our destiny will lift us up.

It is for this reason that there are several kinds of destiny, each with monumental powers. The Creator blesses us with multiple kinds of destiny so that we will appreciate our assignment with destiny when we discover it, and we will use it to serve, lead, and spiritually impact others. Unfortunately the voice of destiny has told us that all humans have sinned; we all come short of the glory of the Creator, who is purpose-driven with the ingenuity and power of destiny. Still, when we harness and use that destiny properly, we become a big light unto smaller lights; a great teacher unto the uninformed; a great provider to the downtrodden.

The use and application of destiny makes us realize how we are ennobled to be in line with the Infinite, in union with the consummate reality. It gives us the power to achieve without limitations.

When this book was bestowed on me to give to the universal family as a gift to posterity, I was stunned. I appreciated it as inspired wisdom, and I understood that when we are in tune with destiny, we are naturally engaged in objective and pragmatic creativity.

As I have come to understand it, the power of destiny manifests itself in the following ways:

- ❑ The power of destiny is the way of honest living.
- ❑ The application of the power of destiny turns one into a seeker of truth.
- ❑ The power of destiny is pure, perfect, practical, purposeful, perpetual, and highly principled.
- ❑ It is the power of ennobled souls who appreciate the wisdom of the living word.
- ❑ When properly discovered and utilized, the power of destiny is life's bedrock, the fountain of living waters.
- ❑ The power of destiny is the force that determines honest success. This is why hones t and successful people are naturally designated as lucky or destined. They are the chosen ones, the ones who become the envy of the world, the challengers of tradition, the missionary apostolate of any society. But they are more than simply conquerors or trailblazers; because anything and everything must obey them.

- The power of destiny is the supreme key that opens heaven, a guide to live a purposeful life, the force and wisdom that should drive the cravings of the soul and the church.
- The power of destiny is the power of prophecy. All humans who are true to themselves, with strict obedience to the Creator, use the power of destiny—not a magic wand, as some people may believe.
- ❏ Jesus Christ was destined to win human salvation, and he accomplished that mission without regrets.
- ❏ Buddha was destined to be the light and teacher of Indians, and he accomplished that mission, despite overbearing colonial rule, without faltering.
- ❏ The Prophet Muhammad was destined to give man the knowledge of the Koran, establishing the Islamic world, and he accomplished that task because the power of destiny was his driving force.
- ❏ Plato was destined to give the universe a philosophical cosmogony, establishing the government of truth in Greece, and he accomplished that mission. Platonic teachings continued even after his mortal body left this universe.
- ❏ Michael Faraday was destined to give the universe an understanding of electromagnetism, and he accomplished this task.
- ❏ Sir Isaac Pitman was destined to give man stenographic writing, which he translated as shorthand, and the fulfillment of this task made his contemporaries look upon him as a genius in monographic and stenographic technology.

In our present stage of the evolution of civilization, A. U. Aliche has become destined with the powers of creative ingenuity, giving the universe an energetic foundation and incubator, the monumental gallery he calls the Cosmic Bible.

Humans have eulogized destiny in words, poems, and songs, as when we sing, "Oh Lord my God, when I in awesome wonder, consider all the works thy hands have made . . ." But that praise is not enough. Apart from extolling the power of destiny, Aliche believes that the discovering and mastering of our destiny reveals why God designated us to the spiritual rank and file, placing us among the blessed angels who were able to recognize and use their celestial assignments with destiny in reverence to God, Christ, and the Holy Spirit. This is why the power of destiny, manifested in balanced creativity, is the supreme power of immortal creations.

Every noble soul must make an honest and purposeful effort to harness, impact, appreciate, and welcome the consummate power of destiny so that at the end of our earthly life, we will rejoice with the angels in heaven. Then we can sing that timeless song:

> Children of the heavenly king,
> As ye journey, sweetly sing;
> Sing your Saviour's worthy praise
> Glorious in his works and ways.
>
> We are traveling home to God
> In the way the fathers trod.
> They are happy, now are we;
> Soon their happiness shall see.
>
> Lift your eyes, ye sons of light!
> Zion city is in sight;
> There our endless home shall be,
> There our Lord we soon shall see.
>
> Fear not, brethren! Joyful stand
> On the borders of your land;
> Jesus Christ, your father's son
> Bid you undismayed go on.
>
> Lord, obedient we would go,
> Gladly leaving all below;
> Only thou our leader be,
> And we still will follow thee.
>
> SSS—838

Think . . .

"Our destiny exercises its influence over us even when, as yet, we have not learnt its nature: it is our future that lays down the law of our today."
Friedrich Nietzsche

"The first evil choice or act is linked to the second; and each one to the one that follows, both by the tendency of our evil nature and by the power of habit, which holds us by a destiny."
Tyron Edwards"

"The power of destiny is your noble power to use and create posterity."
Anthony U. Aliche

Chapter 4

What informed the wisdom and power of destiny, causing it to be purpose-creative?

Many people do not understand the meaning of destiny or its power or wisdom. In particular, they don't understand why its ingenuity is realistically driven in union with purposeful creativity.

If destiny is God in action, with man cooperating with his Creator, it stands to reason that the creative power of destiny is purpose-driven, ingenious, and sequential. Solomon devoted his time to exploring the virtues and values of destiny, ultimately concluding that destiny is God, occurring when man agrees and cooperates absolutely with his Creator.

Have You Discovered Your Assignment with Destiny? can be understood as spiritual enlightenment, a window into the secrets and treasures of wealth. It comprises wisdom in action, inspiration in motion, and enlightenment with focus, revealing why the power of destiny works as quickly as that of the angels.

Authoritatively, the angels are destined to serve, worship, honour, affirm, proclaim, and glorify the authority of God. Man is assigned to follow suit in order to return the same praises to the Almighty Creator.

In this respect, the power and wisdom of destiny are significant in the following ways:

- ❑ Destiny leads us to serve humanity as part of the brotherhood of man.
- ❑ Destiny leads us to be our brother's keeper, not his killer.
- ❑ Destiny leads us to be divine in our actions and reactions, because destiny is authoritatively divine.
- ❑ The power of destiny lies in the strength of its creation, which is why its treasures can be discovered only when man cooperates with the Creator.
- ❑ Its wisdom is famously applied in divine virtues, which is why destiny drives the common virtues that characterise great men.
- ❑ The power of destiny lies in its ability to take us from problems to praises.
- ❑ The power of destiny is the power of light and truth. It is the timeless power of life and love. No human being can give his own destiny to a fellow human being.
- ❑ The power of destiny is the oldest story in creation, but it has remained the youngest wisdom of all ages.
- ❑ Destiny is represented in the immortal scriptures by the authority of the Holy Spirit. The Bible is a manifestation of the authoritative ingenuity and creativity of destiny.
- ❑ Destiny had its cosmic foundation in God's words, "Come let us make man in our own image."
- ❑ Destiny is the electrifying power and embodiment of the biblical verse "Let there be light: and there was light."
- ❑ The wisdom and power of destiny gave rise to the Gospels, particularly John 1:1.
- ❑ "All things bright and beautiful, all creatures great and small" are symbolic creations of destiny. Anyone who studies the structure of the sun, moon, or stars will certainly concur that God is the consummate destiny of all ages.

It is unfortunate that man does not understand the designing power of destiny, its engineering foundation, or the structure of its anatomy. That's why the title of this book comes in the form of a question. It is an admonition, a prayer, a call to communion, encouraging participation in the sacrament of innermost worship.

If Jesus Christ were not destined as the saviour of man, the path by which we can appreciate our destiny in God, human salvation would not have been possible.

This chapter answers most of the questions about destiny that have long bothered man, including how we can discover our assignment with destiny, which is a spiritual prize, a mystical mandate, and the way of life and truth. Destiny answers the age-old question of what lies ahead for mankind. It reveals how we can develop the spiritual urge to know our Creator, whose love and lofty goals for us are boundless, infinite, wonderful, and marvelous.

A look at the mission and activities of Christ's ministry reveals that he came to show us the way to our destiny, which is the glorious call of all humans. In fact, no human being can live a fulfilled life without discovering the wisdom and power of his destiny.

Destiny makes you know and appreciate that when God calls you blessed, when God opens the way, when God labours for you, when God cares for you, when God considers you fit for the purpose of heaven—when you are in tune with the Infinite—any devilish effort to thwart this divine plan will yield only vanity upon vanity.

For the record, this book is spiritually consummated, helping us discover the power and wisdom of destiny, which reveals itself in us from our head to our toes. This is why God designated man, which he created in his destined ingenuity, in his supreme and consummate image.

Think . . .

"Destiny makes you know and appreciate that when God calls you blessed, when God opens the way, when God labours for you, when God cares for you, when God considers you fit for the purpose of heaven—when you are in tune with the Infinite—any devilish effort to thwart this divine plan will yield only vanity upon vanity."
Anthony U. Aliche

Chapter 5

Why is man a subject and object of divine destiny?

It is the intent of this book to make man understand that he is a supreme object and subject of divine destiny, irrevocably intertwined with it the Creator, as the Christian hymn says: "I could not do without thee, oh Saviour of the lost."

Sailors in the Spanish Armada inspired a similar song, "Must I Go Empty-Handed," another poetic acknowledgment of man's dependence on his Creator.

The theme of "I Could Not Do without Thee" reveals the following truths:

- ❖ Man has no authority over himself.
- ❖ Man's creations are in vain when they are not aligned with the power and wisdom of the Creator.
- ❖ We waste time chasing shadows if we do not invite the good Lord to take his position in our life, kindling the power of our destiny.
- ❖ The purpose of our earthly life is to discover our assignment with destiny. We must realize our destiny through honest service to the one-world family and through the use and application of truth, which is in union with our destiny.

The fact that man is both a subject and an object of divine destiny practically and spiritually confirms that God is in man when man desires to be in God by awakening his consciousness.

The use and application of divine destiny enables man to conquer the following ills:

- ❖ fraud
- ❖ mediocrity
- ❖ hatred
- ❖ jealousy
- ❖ obnoxiousness
- ❖ slavery
- ❖ lies
- ❖ spiritual selfishness
- ❖ spiritual weakness
- ❖ adultery and fornication
- ❖ slander
- ❖ covetousness
- ❖ wretchedness
- ❖ wickedness
- ❖ lust

When one is not in union with his destiny, he lives a life of complaints, fault-finding, deception, gossip, and a constant craving for things that do not promote the in-dwelling of the Holy Spirit. We can see the signs of this in our contemporary churches and their leaders.

Since the dawn of consciousness, the great majority of humans have not known that they are ennobled and committed to be living subjects and objects of divine destiny. This lack of knowledge is largely responsible for the chaos in our world, spreading poverty and devilish acts which do not promote our honest and divine destiny. It is this destiny that must be made manifest if man is to be a living and divine image of the Creator.

We've all seen those people who are fond of going to church without going to Christ, going to court without going to the law.

And by avoiding the law, they disobey the course of equity, fair play, and honest transaction. This is why it is important to remind man that he is an object and subject of divine law, which is under the grace of destiny.

This book evolved as another monumental work, a spiritual trailblazer. In essence, it is a great encyclopedia, intended to make us appreciate ourselves, our neighbours, our country, our universe, and our Creator. It is also intended to inspire our own reordering, so that our own objectives align with the reality of destiny. In particular, it extols human life, forever ennobled in the person of Jesus Christ, the divine avatar.

Sadly, we all have sinned and fall short of the glory of the Creator. Ever since sin entered into man through his lustful appetite, he began disobeying himself and the laws of nature. Through this disobedience he became vulnerable to unrealistic inspirations and aspirations, forgetting that he is a living subject and object of destiny. As a result of his disobedience, the Creator told man that He has unchanging standards—that in spite of His loving gift of Christ, He remains a jealous God.

Man is an object and subject of divine nature. Thus Christ stated that with faith we can move mountains, we can provoke the heavens positively, we can do mightier acts and works than He did. But has man recognized the wisdom of faith in destiny, the power, vision, and focus of faith in destiny? Has he anointed himself with the light and the sacrament of destiny?

The time has come for man to withdraw from his oblivion and see himself anew as the embodiment of the beauty of the universe, the purpose of destiny, and the vision and mission of the universe. We will not be forgiven of our sins if we make no effort to discover our assignment with destiny, because its force is a great calling, a spiritual mandate, the ultimate utilization of God's gift. On the strength of its fortified current you can become a teacher, an engineer, a technologist, a scientist, a philosopher, a mathematician, an inventor, an industrialist, a physician, a social worker—all these ennoble you to become a co-creator with the ingenious creative current. This is only achievable when you realize that you are an object and subject of divine destiny, compassionately created not to die, fail, or live in poverty, but to be lifted through the fulfillment of your destiny to the glory of the owner of your life, the one who destined what you would become even when you were in your mother's womb. Destiny defines the womb of a mother as the oracle of creativity.

The same destiny inspired this author to tell the world that every subject of God is an object of Christ, and every object of Christ is an heir to the kingdom of heaven. All subjects and objects of divine destiny are washed with the consummate authority of the destined blood of Christ, who despite being a victim of Calvary, spiritually and physically, became a hero and victor, so that we can ask the laudable questions: *Gethsemane, where are thy powers? Golgotha, where is thy strength? The ephemeral cross and Calvary, where are thy carpenters? Where are those who thought they could crucify and conquer the Light of the world?*

This is why every man must strive to know himself and the purpose for which he was put on this planet. With this knowledge there is a divine assurance which is reflected in a timeless maxim: One with God is majority.

God is our Creator, ennobling us to be His subjects and using Jesus Christ to bless and possess us as His objects. A destined child forever glorifies and praises the work of God and the kingdom of heaven. Destiny informs the wisdom and power of the blessed angels. Greatness can be achieved when we work to discover our assignment with destiny and then work to fulfill the mandate of this assignment.

I could not do without thee,
O saviour of the lost,
Whose precious blood redeemed me
At such tremendous cost:
Thy righteousness, thy pardon,
Thy sacrifice must be
My only hope and comfort,
My glory and my plea.

I could not do without thee,
I cannot stand alone.
I have no strength or goodness,
No wisdom of my own:
But thou, beloved saviour
Art all in all to me,
And weakness will be power
If leaning hard on thee.

I could not do without thee
For years are fleeting fast,
And soon in solemn silence
The river must be passed:
But thou wilt never leave me;
And, though the waves run high,
I know thou wilt be near me,
And whisper, it is I.
SSS 844

Think . . .

"We waste time chasing shadows if we do not ask the good Lord to take his position in our life and rekindle the power of our destiny."
Anthony U. Aliche

"No man can conquer the world without destiny at work."
Anthony U. Aliche

"I believe that the people, instead of pretty lies, should be told the truth, no matter how ugly it may be. What can we do, destiny hasn't been kind to us; but, with the help of God, we will prevail."
Alija Izetbegovic

"The best of academicians do not know the power of destiny. This is why destiny is a born genius."
Anthony U. Aliche

Chapter 6

Has man known these divine facts, which represent great knowledge?

It is important to note that man's inability to understand himself, the miracles and wonders of nature, and the monumental wisdom of destiny remains a challenge which will take him many years to overcome.

The lessons in chapter 5, dealing with the subject of man as the divine alchemy and property of destiny, opened a new horizon of information. The purpose of this revelation is born out of the fact that man is still primordial, still at the level of original civilization.

Any subject and object of divine destiny is ennobled to possess the following qualities:

- ❖ He will be a co-creator with the use of cosmic wisdom.
- ❖ He will be purpose-driven with the use of truthful principles.
- ❖ He will live a life free of negative instincts, dogmas, doctrines, culture, and religion. The spiritual ingenuity of destiny worked as a natural fulcrum supporting the rare work of the Twelve World Teachers.
- ❖ He is usually simple, practical, and objective, and he practices what he preaches. This is why science is spiritually ennobling.

_____

❖ He always cooperates with the Creator, becoming co-creators whose works are born of the immortal foundry of Mother Nature.

Creation does not know that man is a subject and object of destiny, so we make mockery of the truth, lacking the wisdom and ingenuity to be our brother's keeper and to appreciate his values. The nature and structure of destiny, which is an eternal current from God, reveals that man is at an important crossroads regarding the wisdom of balanced knowledge.

It is important to mention in this context that apart from the superhuman Twelve World Teachers, and an enlightened few who were recorded in the annals of cosmic consciousness, humanity and the rest of creation have remained far away from the rays of destiny, from the love of destiny, from the power and force of destiny. To the uninformed, this knowledge of destiny is timidly reflected in the lives of the materially wealthy or the politically or socially powerful, but unfortunately the lives of these humans are never recorded within the objective annals of destiny.

A look at the lives of the Twelve World Teachers, including Christ, Buddha reveals that these humans lived a purpose-driven life, a life of being a universal pacesetter and their brother's keeper. They appreciated the values of creation, thereby understanding and respecting the ingenuity of the super-genius Creator. This is why their legacies, philosophies, doctrines, and contributions to the welfare of humanity continue to sustain us today.

These humans preached and practiced love, peace, understanding, charity, and unity of the whole world. They were never associated with negative actions or transactions like inhumanity, recklessness, corruption, wickedness, or barbarity. These rare souls sought only godly things. They were interested only in developing an organized, fair world province. This is why generation after generation continues to celebrate and remember their immortal contributions.

Man has not known that he is an object and subject of divine destiny because of the enmity and errors of science, technology, engineering, culture, tradition, religion, theology, and ephemeral educational systems that tend to undermine a dynamic, purpose-driven life. The way our religious leaders interpret and teach the scriptures negates many natural spiritual values, the most important of which is destiny.

The question here is, Are all these negative factors a calculated effort to deter the progress of human development?

Most people would say yes. But speaking from my inspired knowledge and objective understanding, I would say that "yes" is not a complete answer. The fact is, these negative acts are performed by criminals and ungodly beings who do not seek the face of God. This is why it has become common practice to loot treasuries in the name of an annual pilgrimage.

The time has come for humanity to understand that everything in creation comes from the authoritative ingenuity of divine destiny. This is why Christ challenged us with the celestial admonition, "With faith in God, you can do greater things than I have done."

With these words, which originate from the destined language of scripture, I hereby conclude that man is still in search of his own spiritual destiny. The only way we can appreciate the spiritual mission of this search is to recognize that we are created as both subjects and properties of destiny. This is what made the Creator define man as His likeness and image, even though the very person exalted to this glorious position forgets that he can do nothing if the Creator does not pave the way for his destiny to be his portion, purpose, dynamic partner, and gardener. To know that we are all eternal, products of the infinite bank of destiny, is the best knowledge we can have, reminding us that a child of destiny is the greatest gift to humanity.

Think . . .

"Creation does not know that man is a subject and object of destiny, so we make mockery of the truth, lacking the wisdom and ingenuity to be our brother's keeper and to appreciate his values."

"Destiny is the foundation of the divine current. It is the divine thinker of all eras."
A. U. Aliche

Chapter 7

Have you discovered your destiny?

A lot of people are living a life of no vision, no focus, and no understanding. Many don't understand the concept of destiny, which does not even enter their thoughts.

Have You Discovered Your Assignment with Destiny? is a clarion call for man to awaken; a challenge for man to pick himself up; a trailblazing command for man to reflect on the purpose, mission, and philosophy of life. This chapter, written with the guidance of consummate inspiration, will answer other important questions, like . . .

- ❖ Is destiny real?
- ❖ Am I destined for anything?
- ❖ Have I discovered my destiny?
- ❖ What are the obstacles to my fulfilling this destiny?
- ❖ What can I do to discover my destiny?
- ❖ Who among my contemporaries have discovered their destiny?
- ❖ Why is destiny defined as God in action, with man in objective and spiritual cooperation with the Creator?

These and similar questions serve as a wake-up call, an admonition, a spiritual reminder that you must discover your assignment with destiny.

It is important to realize that the rewards and motivations that lead us to academic excellence or professional eminence do not conform to the divine directives of destiny. Unlike those man-made contests, destiny is real. It is a mighty ocean, a co-creator, a consummate achiever, as powerful and wonderful as the North Star, as glorious and dynamic as the wisdom of the West. Destiny is ingenious, revealing the omnipotence of God in all creation.

If you ask a roadside mechanic whether he has discovered his assignment with destiny, he will likely answer yes, because he has a job that puts food on his table. He doesn't know whether that is his destiny, or what his gifted destiny is.

Often people find themselves in certain jobs, professions, or schools because of poverty, lack of influence, or problems with their environment and government, including oppressive social policies. This is why the following advice should be considered a mandate:

- Always strive to seek your destiny, for therein lies your covenant with the Creator.
- Always strive to appreciate the destiny of others; by so doing, you will increase the chances of harnessing your own destiny.
- A wicked and envious person can never see the light of destiny, because destiny is pure, perfect, practical, dynamic, and objective. When destiny is finally harnessed and used well, it results in miraculous wonders—evidence that God is its author and foundation.
- We must learn how to be careful, how to be our brother's keeper, and how to give from the abundance of our heart. Take as an example the scriptural story of the Samaritan who saw and helped somebody at the height of need.
- We must understand that destiny is the Bible of the soul, the craft of the mind, and the wisdom that propels honest life, although its manifestation is always called "luck."
- We must strive to appreciate and practice honest transactions in our daily life. This book implores you to make a quest for honesty, reordering and adjusting your

lifestyle and confessing all your past actions which were not in agreement with divine laws.
- *Have You Discovered Your Assignment with Destiny?* always directs us to look at our past as well as our future, considering what is right in order to confirm if we are in tune with the Infinite.

The power of destiny, with its divine purpose, transcends all laws, creeds, dogmas, and doctrines, all ephemeral and un-objective philosophy. It transcends husband and wife, and it especially transcends culture, with its traditions of religion and church.

Those who conclusively answered the question, Have you discovered your assignment with destiny? are case studies of people with universal understanding. Their minds were watered with special knowledge; they were seers for all ages; they were gurus whose wisdom came from destiny's bank of celestial knowledge. So the question for you is, Are you fit and worthy to be named among these souls, who lived their lives according to the destiny of immortality?

> *Have You Discovered Your Assignment with Destiny? is always remembering, reminding us of, and confirming the scriptural warning, "All have sinned and run short of the glory of the Creator."*

This statement is difficult to hear, but it is very motivating to humans who believe that we can achieve our assignment with destiny. Any man who must discover his assignment with destiny takes his guidance directly from nature—not from the wells of man, but from the wells of the Holy Spirit. Such a person is in constant touch with the heavens; he is always at peace with his soul and mind. His life always serves to glorify its source, the wisdom of knowledge of his destiny, and he is always labeled as a pioneer destined for a graced land.

I could say much more in this chapter, but instead I will summarize it with comprehensive and inspired words which can translate into song, poetry, philosophy, or even an inscription:

> *The day of the Lord in the life of a man, woman, family, community, society, country, or universe starts on that glorious day when one discovers his assignment with destiny.*

This is why this book was written, to cure the blindness that has prevented you from seeking the real purpose of your own destiny. It will help you make a glorious contribution to the world rather than simply being a receiver and taker. When we discover our assignment with destiny, we will be gladdened by the knowledge that "In my father's house are many mansions."

Think . . .

"The day of the Lord in the life of a man, woman, family, community, society, country, or universe starts on that glorious day when one discovers his assignment with destiny."
Anthony U. Aliche

"Serendipity. Look for something, find something else, and realize that what you've found is more suited to your needs than what you thought you were looking for."
Lawrence Block

"Dreams are like stars . . . you may never touch them, but if you follow them they will lead you to your destiny."
Anonymous

"I seldom end up where I wanted to go, but almost always end up where I need to be."
Douglas Adams

Chapter 8

How have you used your destiny for creative achievement?

St. Germaine, who is known as the father of alchemy, used nature's ingenious technology to practice self-engineering and—transformation. He gave to the world his immortal wisdom in the science of alchemy, including a wonderful biography of Mother Nature. St. Germaine concluded his anointed and destined works with a glorious discussion of "fraternal immortality."

This chapter is a reminder to you that you were not put on this earth to tell lies or engage in mischievous or greedy acts. You are not here to advance the cause of indiscipline, kidnapping, terrorism, or the murder of innocent souls, of trailblazers who are destined to set the world on a course of ingenious balance.

When I read in the scriptures that God cannot be mocked, and that He is a jealous God, I am always reminded of the confession of David when he unlawfully took Uriah's wife. His open confession is contained in Psalm 51, but even with that, God could not withhold his wrath in punishing David.

Your presence on earth is by the doing of the Creator, and your purpose is not to defile the glorious face of the universe. You are not to use your material wealth to terrorize, intimidate, or malign others, or to destroy the less privileged—a practice seen throughout humanity, particularly in third-world countries.

Instead, destiny calls you to a humane, purposeful life, which includes the following mandates and laws:

- You have a mandate to serve the universe with the gift of nature's resources.
- You are called to be your brother's keeper, following the principles of the brotherhood of man.
- Destiny is the consummation of the Ten Commandments, which nurtured and inspired all philosophical codes of ethics.
- Destiny is the foundation of the Sermon on the Mount, which designated Christ as the garden of destiny, the celebrated Rose of Sharon, the destined child of the universe. This is why Buddha proclaimed that the whole world would become a heaven when humans applied with spiritual understanding all the tenets contained within the Sermon on the Mount, especially the Beatitudes.

I refer all who read this book to the immortal concepts in Matthew 5.

Solomon also had great insights about God and destiny and about man and destiny, as written in Ecclesiastes and Proverbs. Ecclesiastes, especially, provides a timeless answer to the question, How have you used your destiny for creative achievement?

For further examination of this subject, I often refer people to other of my works, which are destined to inspire them to live according to the purpose of their creation and to understand why the Almighty created them. These books include the following:

- *Challenge Is a Catalyst to Success*
- *What Makes Great Men*
- *From Problems to Praises*
- *Whose Vessel Are You*
- *Favour Favours the Brave*

- *God's Gifts Are Irrevocable*
- *Using Your Gifts to Help Others*

I also refer people to other select books, like *Women Are the Aroma of Beauty*, which teaches that with love, all works are easy, and that when God calls you blessed, no man can curse you.

Many people do not yet know that the power, purpose, and wish of the Creator—as well as the teaching of Christ, which called for our destiny to be in spiritual alignment—is for us to desire one-world purpose and achieve universal love. We are called to apply the spiritual principles of peace and harmony, using our destined wealth and riches to uplift others and make the downtrodden know that God cares about them.

You must not allow any day to pass without somebody saying "thank you" to you for what he has benefited from you—financially, materially, physically, or mentally.

How have you used your destiny to benefit others? You must use the powers of destiny to reach out and bless others and to praise the Lord. In doing so, you will attract the blessings of the heavens, from which all blessings come.

When I was initially inclined to write on this subject, my intuition—which I felt as if it were an electric current—first manifested itself as inspiration. That inspiration drove my desire to approach the messenger of destiny, the Holy Spirit. In the company of the Holy Spirit, who knows how to talk to Christ, the wisdom of all ages, I accepted that this book would be written under divine instruction. God with his grace would provide the flavour, the rhythm, the systematic structure, the natural talent, and the wording. This is why my next chapter—"Whom have you benefited or helped with your destiny?"—is a glorious achievement which the ordinary man would classify as a masterpiece.

The Twelve World Teachers used their destiny to give the whole world a purposeful culture and traditions, including religion, education, science, engineering, technology, and graceful provisions. This is why we continue to celebrate their achievements, which formed a lasting foundation that is both missionary in nature and apostolic in practice.

Other transfigured immortals include William Shakespeare, Jacob Boehm, Sir Isaac Pitman, Sir Isaac Newton, Albert Einstein, Euclid, Galileo, Michael Faraday, Plato, Socrates, Pythagoras, Emmanuel Kant, Dr. Walter Russell, Lord Krishna, Herbert Spencer Louise, H. A. Clement, L. Durell, and the fathers of physics, Nelkon and Abbot.

The ingenious father of modern anatomy, Sir Andrew, is known as a purpose-driven human who used his destiny to achieve a lot for humanity. He ensured that the creations born from his destiny were permanently recorded in the annals of human history and evolution.

The day you discover your assignment with destiny begins a new Sabbath, a new communion, a new mandate, and a new ordination to a purposeful life aligned with the heavens. All this is a must: you will create a grace-filled land that glorifies Almighty God, who has given humans the anointing of His destiny, countries the benefit of His destiny, and continents the wonders of His destiny.

The lessons of this chapter can be summed up in a simple sentence, which is a wake-up call to service, knowledge, and wisdom. It is both a spiritual mandate and a call to communion, and when we strictly adhere to its tenets, the purpose and joys of our earthly life will be found in the immortality of our achievements. This chapter simply asks you to start now serving the world with the objective wealth of your assignment with destiny.

Fill thou my life, O Lord my God,
In every part with praise,
That my whole being may proclaim
Thy being and thy way.
Not for the lip of praise alone
Nor e'en the praising heart,
I ask, but for all a life made up
Of praise in every part:

Praise in the common things of life,
Its goings out and in;
Praise in each duty and each deed,
However small and mean.

Fill every part of me with praise:
Let all my being speak,
Of thee and of thy love, of thy love O Lord
Poor though I be and weak.

So shalt thou, Lord, receive from me
The praise and glory due you:
And so shall I begin on earth
The song forever new.

So shall each fear, each fret, each care,
Be turned into song;
And every winding of the way
The echo shall prolong.

So shall no part of day or night
Un-bless our common being;
But all my life, in every step
Be fellowship with thee.

Hymn Book—604
(Methodist Church Nigeria)

Think . . .

"The power, purpose, and wish of the Creator—as well as the teaching of Christ, which called for our destiny to be in spiritual alignment—is for us to desire one-world purpose and achieve universal love. We are called to apply the spiritual principles of peace and harmony, using our destined wealth and riches to uplift others and make the downtrodden know that God cares about them."
Anthony U. Aliche

"A great revolution in just one single individual will help achieve a change in the destiny of a society and, further, will enable a change in the destiny of humankind."
Daisaku Ikeda

Chapter 9

Whom have you benefited through the use and application of your destiny?

This chapter can be defined as a practical and perfect assessment of what you have done for others—for humanity and all creation—with the blessings the Creator has lavished upon you. These blessings are destiny driven, given and re-given. Destiny has an eternal law of balanced giving and re-giving, a law whose authoritative concepts underpinned the Sermon on the Mount.

Observe that within our villages and communities, one man might live in a duplex while others around him are living in thatched and mud houses. The same man might even have built duplexes for his girlfriends and family members, not understanding that his actions are not in accordance with the laws of destiny.

In Third World countries, politicians and successful businessmen will even subject their wards and relations to torture and poverty in order to avoid being challenged. But God is vested with the power of reminding man of his sins when man has forgotten them.

If you are a human hoping to embody God's image, ask yourself these questions:

- Whom have I benefited from my destiny?
- What do people say about me?

- What opinion do people have of me?
- Do I have more enemies than friends—and if so, why?

These are important and enlightening questions which must certainly make you reflect, and even worry.

When it comes to material wealth, money behaves rather like a newborn baby. I'm reminded of a wonderful maxim: *Money has no master; money does not make things; money is a passing shadow.* But the uninformed, in their ignorance, believe that *Money makes the man.*

In fact, many people have no regard for the material welfare of their brothers and sisters, neighbours and friends. They won't bother to help them even when they have excess to share.

Look at what is happening in most countries of the world: their leaders have shown that human wickedness is actually the greatest exterminator of life. But wickedness will destroy them and their families; the scriptures have made it clear that righteousness exalts a nation, while sin brings reproach.

Our quality of life determines what happens to us. Our ability to give brings consummate blessings to us. When people say, "God bless you," or "Well done," or when they bless your children, they are acknowledging that they have benefited from your destiny.

When Manly Palmer Hall wrote his highly illuminating work, *American Assignment with Destiny*, this anointed philosopher/mystic never realized that the theme of his book reflected the American motto, In God We Trust.

This motto inspires America to reach out as a helper to other nations; to strengthen the course of good leadership and democracy; to use the wealth of its wisdom and physical enrichment to change the course of the universe; and to fight on behalf of the downtrodden. The destined manner with which former President Bill Clinton initiated and universally propagated the concept of America's visa

---

lottery was a lasting contribution to the world. His use of destiny should be a challenge to you and to the whole human race.

Uncle Nelson Mandela, our apostolate emeritus whom I have always considered the Christ of South Africa, utilized the ingenuity of destiny to fight for the that country's liberation from the shackles of the wicked British government.

Today, the whole world celebrates the achievements of Nelson Mandela, Bill Clinton, and others who have in one way or another benefited humans though the consummate wisdom and wealth of their destiny.

At this point, it is imperative that you answer the following questions:

- Whom have you benefited through the use and application of your destiny?
- To what level do these benefits glorify and thank Almighty God?
- Are these benefits temporary or permanent?
- Why are you using your destiny to make loans to people, even when you know they are not capable of paying you back?
- Why are you using your destined opportunities to enslave others, destroying and impoverishing them?
- Do you know that God brings change to humans when they least expect it?
- Do you know that the poorest man today can be the wealthiest man tomorrow—perhaps becoming the person who will save you and your family?
- What are the benefits of wicked and dishonest acts like indiscipline, corruption, and inhumanity?

These questions are very important because many people do not understand the principles of honest service and honest help. The time has come for us to desire to love one another and serve one another through our destiny. For it is clearly stated in the scriptures that givers do not lack and that the hand that gives is permanently uplifted. Whoever benefits the world with the use and application of his destiny remains a celebrated hero. Of course, it must be stated that for one to be a leader of a people, he must also accept the position of chief servant of the people.

The people who are most celebrated and highly remembered all over the world are those who have made a positive impact with their wisdom, their ingenuity and creativity, their knowledge and education, and their service to the universal family, which comes naturally through the application of their destiny. That is why I celebrate destiny as the father of honest service and the ingenious mother of many famous humans.

Any human who refuses to benefit others with the use and application of his destiny makes a permanent and irrevocable case against himself, his family, and his relations, because the natural purpose of destiny is to be discovered and utilized so that we become partners with the Creator as co-creators, and objective and pragmatic partners with nature.

When we benefit others through the application of our destiny, we are simply and humbly telling God, "Thank you for making me a unique and immortal creation, using my destiny objectively and positively for your glory." Your destined acts glorify the wonders of the Creator just as in rhythm and rhyme the blessed angels worship the Creator. This is why every day of our lives, we should ask ourselves this question: *Whom have I benefited with the glorious gift of my wealth and wisdom?*

Think . . .

"Our ability to give brings consummate blessings to us. When people say, 'God bless you,' or 'Well done,' or when they bless your children, they are acknowledging that they have benefited from your destiny."
Anthony U. Aliche

"Nothing brings me more happiness than trying to help the most vulnerable people in society. It is a goal and an essential part of my life—a kind of destiny. Whoever is in distress can call on me. I will come running wherever they are."
Princess Diana

"The hand that gives is destined to be on top, and givers are destined for more success and greater achievements."
Anthony U. Aliche

Chapter 10

Why do some people waste their destiny rather than using it to live an honest, purpose-driven life?

A look at the call and mission of destiny will reveal that many a man has not been able to use his destiny wisely, consciously, or profitably. This book is best intended to help resolve that problem by reordering human intelligence.

There are many reasons for unenlightened practices that do not promote growth and do not involve practical and studious learning. In fact, a lot of people are busy fooling themselves about their destiny for one of the following reasons:

- They don't make an honest effort.
- They do not put their vision into positive action.
- They are afraid to accept positive challenges.
- They have too much pride (which, as it is said, goes before a fall)
- They are simply unable to live a determined life.
- They lack an education that can stimulate the rekindling of the practice of destiny.
- They practice mundane acts.
- They are not able or willing to place God first—and destiny is God in action, requiring man to cooperate with his Creator.
- Their egocentric appetites lead them to dangerous habits that do not promote the harmonious realization of destiny.

- They practice wickedness, including inhumanity to their fellow man, which is always a setback to the realization of destiny.
- Their actions and transactions are not spiritually driven; destiny is spiritual.
- They are slow to understand the true mystic principles that must be accepted and reckoned with for destiny to be harnessed. Chief among them is the biblical injunction, "Righteousness exalts a nation while sin is a reproach to any people."

The destined assignment of Christopher Columbus, whose achievements are greatly anticipated in the Book of Isaiah's passages about the discovery of the New World, teaches us the following lessons with spiritual revelations:

- We must be steadfast in adhering to the will and wisdom of God.
- We must avoid imitating others at the expense of undoing our destiny.
- God must be trusted and strictly obeyed. This lesson is clear in the stories of figures like David, Joseph, Joshua, and Abraham.
- We must learn how to worship God rather than man.
- We must understand that challenges, difficulties, and tempests are actually blessings, because at the end of the road, there is always a shining star.
- We must learn how to worship with wisdom, with nature, with destiny, and with the Holy Spirit, as the Bible clearly states, "Those that wait upon the Lord shall renew their strength."

Our contemporary statesmen and—women should study the case of the destined Christopher Columbus, as well as those of Benjamin Franklin, Mahatma Gandhi, and George Washington.

A look at the immortal achievements of humans who decided not to be foolish in the quest to actualize their destiny reveals that nothing can be achieved, particularly as it affects destiny, without a price. Often it involves costly tarrying, and it is dependent upon grace, which must be driven and designed by the Creator. This is why evidence abounds that very few humans have been able to actualize the vision of their destiny since the dawn of consciousness.

It's a blessing that *Have You Discovered Your Assignment with Destiny?* comes at this time, when humanity appears to be stagnating at a crossroads; when evil has eaten into the fabric of the universe; when intelligence appears to be eroding; when adherence to the principles of the brotherhood of man appears to be a thing of the past; when the ancient wisdom, "Man, know thyself," seems to be a fairytale. Worst of all, our contemporary systems—even our educational systems—are no longer driven by truth, humility, politeness, understanding, and wisdom. Humans have dangerously jettisoned practical knowledge from their lives. That is the reason for this urgent call to reorder the thinking of man, whose character and desire for honest service lie in studiously working towards realizing his roots and fulfilling his destiny.

Chapters 7 and 8 greatly emphasize using your destiny to enrich others. Without reservation, the author has steadily maintained that on any day that we fail to bless others, we are naturally and spiritually indebted, and we must balance that accumulated debt with a credit.

The wisdom of destiny has emphatically revealed that man's foolishness has remained his greatest obstacle in attaining higher grounds; conquering greater enemies; achieving greater exploits; and understanding the wisdom of the Creator. If we must live in accordance with the directives of Mother Nature, which are destiny-driven, involving love, kindness, charity, and peace, our lives and actions must in turn synchronize with the objective balance of nature's rhythmic essence and ecstasy. The time has come for humanity to stop its myopic actions and forego its erroneous understanding of nature, its lack of reverence for and patronage of nature, and its unwillingness to be a brother's keeper. Destiny daily implores us to desist from foolishness, to stop wasting our precious time. That is why it is the mission of this humble chapter to welcome all humans to be progressive partners with the wisdom of destiny, to partake of the consummate teachings and rhythms of destiny. For there is no other way your love can be fulfilled.

From time eternal, destiny has sought co-partners, people she will use as friends and vessels. She does this so that humanity appreciates her joy and wisdom, the only authority that can reduce foolishness, pride, ego, waste, stagnation, and other ills that do not promote the cause of human character, development, and progress. This helps ensure that we are aligned with destiny's wish, will, and wisdom, which inspired the Creator to design us as His composite, made in his purposeful image.

Think . . .

What could have happened to the New World if Columbus had not embraced the challenges of his destiny?

Christopher Columbus
Italian-born explorer Christopher Columbus broke with tradition in 1492, sailing west in an attempt to find a shorter route to India and China. Basing his calculations for the journey on biblical scripture, Columbus departed from Palos de la Frontera, Spain, on the first of several voyages to what he later called the "New World."

Columbus Sets Sail in 1492
In 1492, explorer Christopher Columbus departed on his first journey in search of a quicker route to Asia. On this voyage Columbus encountered the islands which became known as the West Indies, in the Caribbean Sea. Ferdinand V and Isabella, the king and queen of Castile, sponsored his first expedition.
Microsoft (R) Encarta 2009

Think . . .

"I believe that the earthly Paradise lies here, which no one can enter except by God's leave. I believe that this land which your Highnesses have commanded me to discover is very great, and that there are many other lands in the south of which there have never been reports."
Christopher Columbus (1451-1506)

"If we must live in accordance with the directives of Mother Nature, which are destiny-driven, involving love, kindness, charity, and peace, our lives and actions must in turn synchronize with the objective balance of nature's rhythmic essence and ecstasy."
Anthony U. Aliche

"I never worry about action, but only about inaction."
Winston Churchill

"They were seeking out the treasure of their destiny, without actually wanting to live out their destiny."
Paulo Co Pelho

Chapter 11

What are the purpose and the philosophy of Africa's assignment with destiny, if any?

It is unfortunate that one of the most populous continents in the universe, named "Africa" by the aboriginal Gnostics, has not yet discovered its assignment with destiny, with Mother Nature, and with science. The worst outcome of this situation is that African countries like Nigeria, Liberia, Botswana, and Rwanda have fought civil wars and had international disputes. The menace of inhumane cultures and traditions, as well as religious melancholy, has taken its toll on Africa's psyche, which appears to be critically stagnant at what should be its takeoff point in harnessing and realizing her assignment with destiny.

A high level of racism, which was predominant in apartheid-era South Africa, appears to be one of the colonial and dehumanizing strategies of the white race, particularly Britain, to keep Africa stagnant, insulated from the positive lure of knowledge, understanding, and wisdom. When the white race brought missionaries to Africa under the auspices of evangelization, our people were not aware that the missions introduced an indirect form of slavery whose aim was to isolate and concentrate industrial activities for the benefit of Britain.

It is pathetic that up until now, Africa has not established a university of natural science, a university of humanities, a natural science foundation, or an incubator of natural research. The intellectual stagnation within this continent leads one to believe that neither our leaders nor their followers have been able to draw an acceptable and inspired blueprint to harness our assignment with destiny.

Is it not an irony that countries like Japan, China, Korea, and Malaysia, which came to Nigeria and collected our natural resources, are gradually outgrowing the label of "Third World country"?

Is it not a pity that our abundance of natural resources—minerals that the white race has conspired to use in order to impoverish us—is wasted daily?

What can our leaders tell us about the kidnapping, armed robbery, terrorism, government instability, corruption, indiscipline, immorality, and the social and religious instability that have harmed the continent?

Is it not unfortunate that this continent suffers from civil melancholy and social and traditional vices resulting from the fact that our leaders are not focused; that they lack spiritual vision; they are not in tune with the Infinite; that their minds and thoughts are not driven by spiritual ideals?

What are we telling the world and the Creator when our educational system, our industry, and our commerce have decayed beyond words, although we still don't feel the pain of living like lame ducks?

All these questions call to mind Alan Paton's immortal work, *Cry the Beloved Country*. In this book, the product of a divine mandate, the author weeps for the highly favoured continent which has refused to appreciate God; to know the values of truth; to empower its youth; and to drop its high investment in arms and weapons.

He equally weeps for the exploitation of the continent's natural resources, including gold in Ghana; crude and palm oils, groundnut, cocoa, hides, and skins in Nigeria; bitumen in South Africa, Tanzania, Uganda, and other countries; and surplus crude in Cameroon and Upper Volta.

Is it not a shame that Africa is considered the poorest continent in the world?

With God's mercy and blessing, time will heal the self-imposed tortures and agonies this continent is passing through.

This chapter is highly important to this book because it imparts the following lessons:

- Africa must discover and fulfill her assignment with destiny.
- The time has come to say no to civil wars, injustice, corruption, and other vices that breed political instability.
- Africa's assignment with destiny is a task that must be fulfilled. When civilization began in Egypt, it was divinely inspired, but unfortunately, several factors corrupted its progress: our stupidity and greed; the unnecessary dogma intertwined with our culture and traditions; our disrespect of Mother Nature, which made us cede our highly begotten civilization to the white race, which subjected us to enslavement and, ultimately, oblivion. This is another cry to the beloved continent.

This is another woe which will take millennia to heal, because when God gave Christ to the world, he intended for Africa, first and foremost, to appreciate the wisdom of this celestial gift. It is unfortunate that Africans regressed to various forms of idol worship.

It is Mother Nature's plan and design that Africa should rise to the top of the mountain. Glorious Africans like Nelson Mandela, whom I call "the Christ of South Africa" in my book *Challenge is a Catalyst to Success*, shows that our continent has an eternal and monumental assignment with destiny.

Study the lives of such gentle Gnostics as Sir Kwame Nkrumah of Ghana, Albert Bongo of Gabon, Mugabe of Uganda, and Sir Aminu Kano of Nigeria, and you will see that the virtue of greatness is part of nature's assignment to Africa; it is inherent in the destiny of Africa. This chapter must conclude that the African continent is destined for the following qualities of greatness:

- to be a leader rather than a follower
- to be a provider rather than a beggar
- to be a producer rather than a consumer
- to be highly educated in all human and spiritual endeavours
- to build a museum for the apostolic foundation of truth, which is why nature endowed Africa with countless and monumental resources, including excellent weather and abundant and diverse vegetation and forests
- to better use its fertile land, another wonderful gift of destiny coupled with temperate and calm weather.

Africa is the only continent in the world that enjoys all the gifts of Mother Nature. But unfortunately, her leaders do not know that the advanced continents covet those resources. The result of this envy is clearly shown in the activities of entities like the International Monetary Fund, the World Bank, and the United Nations.

The time has come for Africa, as a continent, to ask itself these questions:

- How old is our civilization?
- What is our symbol and identity?
- What have we achieved during the contemporary era?
- Why are we enemies of our brothers, and what benefits have we derived from fighting wars?
- Why are we stunted in growth, in ideas, and in education?
- Why is the white race always using us as a testing ground?
- How and why have we allowed ourselves to remain slaves within the universal race?
- Why is corruption visibly seen, known, and discussed as part of African society?
- Why are we living a borrowed life, which is not in the nature of our destiny?
- Why have we not been able to develop an acceptable educational system with sound policies and principles?

- Why is Africa a dumping ground for substandard goods and services?
- Why are the nations so hungry and totally dependent even when they have everything it takes to be independent?
- Why have we not asked God to grant us the luminous grace that will help us discover our assignment with destiny, like Asian countries such as Japan, India, China, Malaysia, Korea, and the United Arab Emirates?
- Why haven't we been able to imitate and emulate the industrial and technological wonders of the United States of America, which is known as a world power in creativity, invention, investments, commerce, industry, education, engineering, science, and technology, and which has effectively harnessed the resources of Mother Nature?
- Why is Africa not able to imitate the wonderful conquests and achievements of Germany, France, Russia, Thailand, Greece, Norway, Belgium, Italy, Sweden, and the United Kingdom, known all over the world as empires of universal logic?

It is unfortunate that Africa is living a life separate from nature, truth, God, love, peace, harmony, beauty, and understanding. The mission of the Economic Community of West African States (ECOWAS) and the African Union (AU) appears to be digging more graves for the development of Africa. That is why in order to answer the call of Africa's assignment with destiny, this book is advising that all leopards must turn into golden birds, and all golden birds must strive to conquer the world by applying our ennobled assignment with destiny. This can be possible only when we desire and determine to cooperate with the Creator; to appreciate the values and virtues of love; and to reject indecent and detrimental foreign ideas, concepts, and inventions.

Africa's assignment with destiny, if actualized, will tell the world that the foremost friend of Africa is Jesus, while God, because of His love and trust for Africa, blessed us with abundant gifts: able-bodied humans; monumental resources; great mountains, deserts, and forests; countless oil wells; and plantations rich with palms, plantains, bananas, cocoa, oranges, groundnuts, carrots, onions, rice, beans, cucumbers, peppers, etc.

Consider God's blessings on Africa and how we have fared over the years. Even the deaf and blind realize that Africa has not discerned its assignment with destiny. That is why our progress has stagnated.

For us to move forward, we must look at the motto of the United States, In God We Trust. The wisdom of this motto certainly explains why America is a world power. This is why for Africa to attain a level of development that will make us the envy of other nations, we must understand and appreciate the wisdom of unity; we must be our brother's keeper; and we must develop a united motto.

I would suggest that the motto should read, "Only in God can Africa discover and realize its assignment with destiny."

It is important to point out that from Cape Verde to Cape Town, from Cameroon to Nigeria, from Gambia to Sudan, we have been greatly devastated by civil wars, unfair laws, and detrimental ideas. For example, is it not pathetic that the case of the Bakassi Peninsula, which Nigeria and Cameroon could have settled amicably between them, was decided at the Hague? It was a loss to both Nigeria and Cameroon, while profiting the white race, which provided the weaponry with which Nigeria fought Biafra and with which Biafra retaliated, although unsuccessfully.

Soon, I will write a comprehensive work on Africa's assignment with destiny, and the main thrust of that book will be to provide an expansive blueprint for Africa's future and to teach African countries and their leaders to recognize that the white race cannot develop us, that they cannot give us the magic of their own growth and civilization. The book will be an eye-opener that will help a lot of African leaders stop the dangerous tradition of siphoning their country's economy for the betterment of the white race.

In the immortal words of Sunny Okosun, the great musician who through his art constantly propagated the message of peace in

Africa, "I am waiting for the rainy day when the Black man will rule the world." It is unfortunate that this musical legend did not live to see how Mother Nature blessed the election of Barack Obama, who rose from Kenyan ancestry to become president of the largest democratic country in the world.

This election was a divine sign that Africa has an assignment with destiny, even though it has been delayed. It certainly will happen, if only because no human being has the power to stop the electric currents of destiny and determined mandate. That is why I've taken it upon myself to write this book—to inform all and sundry that Africa as a continent was created as a "graced land," a special province, a gifted continent. Knowing that truth, we must always remember, honour, and appreciate Mama Africa in the persons of Miriam Makeba, Margaret Ekpo, Winnie Mandela, and other notable contributors to motherhood as part of the yet-to-be accomplished task of discovering our assignment with destiny.

I will conclude this chapter with an important admonition:

> *Oh thou beloved continent, which is born from the anatomy of Mother Nature, be guided and directed to know that your destiny is in your hands; to recognize that your over-dependence on the white race will only result in your mortgaging your destiny to them. In order to live up to the glory of our destiny, we must utilize the foundation, the understanding, the meaning and purpose of Africa to bless God with each passing day. We must give our youths a positive, supportive environment so they will fully understand that they are the trustees of posterity. Most important, we must reverse the trend toward Western-orchestrated ideas, learning to live in cooperation with the Creator, whose vested wisdom is the only knowledge that will help us discover our assignment with destiny as a continent, as individuals, and as a blessed region. This is why we must start now—for tomorrow might be too late.*

Think . . .

"I would suggest that our motto should read, 'Only in God can Africa discover and realize its assignment with destiny.'"

"Africa is the only continent in the world that enjoys all the gifts of Mother Nature."
Anthony U. Aliche

"Our destinies are absolutely intertwined. Africa is absolutely fundamental for the South African economy."
Alec Erwin

Chapter 12

What practical lessons are to be derived from this assignment?

Challenge is a catalyst to success, and only challenge, when properly utilized, understood, and harnessed, is capable of bringing change. Challenge and change are simultaneously involved with destiny. Many people do not understand why they must strive with great spiritual desire to discover their destiny.

In one of his most inspired homilies, St. Francis stated that "every man must strive to discover his destiny; to appreciate the purpose for which he is destined in the way and manner that baffles the thinking of others."

With those words in mind, this chapter will build on the theme of the last, which outlined the lapses and demerits of the African continent that have prevented it from discovering its assignment with destiny, despite glorious assets bestowed by the Creator.

There are several practical lessons that are important for Africa and other underdeveloped nations of the world to learn. Among them:

- Destiny is not transferable. Educated people understand that it is the ingenious product of technological development.
- Destiny is indeed a spiritual sparkplug, an electrical current which ignites the genius inherent in everyone.

- Destiny is the only factor that, when understood, makes us live in tune with the glorious powers of eternity.
- When properly harnessed and utilized, destiny makes us co-creators with God. That is why discovering our destiny is the key to our immortality.
- Destiny empowers us to be universal thinkers.
- Destiny is an ingenious force because it drives us to act cosmically, ensuring that man's true wisdom is exposed, expressed, and utilized for the service of others.
- Destiny can never be purchased with money, but the means of its achievement can be acquired. This is why the tools and tricks of the white race are always being purchased by the black race.
- Destiny speaks volumes about one's relationship with the Creator, making a man, a nation, or a system live and look large.
- We are challenged to look beyond our shadows, striving to emulate the founding fathers of destined creativity.
- The lessons here, when properly harnessed, turn us into teachers of truth, makers of great things, luminous images of our Creator. Such people hear the language of inspiration, the language of the Holy Spirit. When the scriptures tell us to "seek, ask, knock," they are encouraging us to discover our destiny, to realize our own ingenuity, to appreciate what it means to be human.
- Destiny, the foundation and fulcrum of consummate creativity, directs us to act positively and behave wonderfully. The character of destiny is embodied in love, peace, harmony, understanding, and creativity. It blends all the features and tenets of a focused life, imparting luminous knowledge only to those who have discovered their assignments with destiny.

It is sad that so many people wallow in abject poverty—material, mental, spiritual, social, and even moral poverty. Every human, every country and continent must strive to discover its assignment with destiny, for there is no other way the long-term developmental goals of the global family can be actualized.

The benefit of destiny is that when you've discovered it, you know that you have arrived; you become accepted and honoured, like an iroko tree; your contemporaries see you as blessed, highly gifted, and unique—a lucky person.

The use and application of the lessons of destiny help our luck shine. They help us glorify the Creator. That is why the discovery of our destiny has remained our greatest task since the dawn of consciousness, with only a few humans—and even fewer countries—accomplishing that task.

For the record, no human, country, or continent can discover its assignment with destiny without God, who is the celestial light from heaven. When the Creator bestows His grace on a human, a country, or a continent, the byproducts are open heavens, a high level of industrialization and technological growth, and great discoveries in the areas of science and technology. This is why the immeasurable contributions of oriental wizards like the Gnostics and the Gideons aligned perfectly and naturally with divine destiny.

For Africa to move forward in discovering its assignment with destiny, it must cut the umbilical cord of idol worship; false dogmas, cultures, traditions, and creeds, and the belief that our help must come from the white race, all should be put aside.

Even though this chapter primarily focuses on the problems outlined in the previous chapter, it's important to note that inspiration, in its wisdom, has also generated many great discoveries, teachings, lessons, and powers that will help Africa and its citizenry think objectively and to act universally.

Now is the time for our great scholars, if they are to live up to their claims, to develop a blueprint for restructuring, reordering, and rediscovering the lost glories of Africa. This way we will surge into nature's wealth of magnanimous wisdom, a font of destiny with the enviable blessings and glories that Mother Nature bestowed upon us. Discovering our assignment with destiny is not just a task for the leaders, the followers, or the youth, but a common mandate in which we all must be involved. If we aren't, we shall continue to live as puppets or slaves. And that is not the desire of our destiny, but an act stemming from our willingness to accept a life of mediocrity—which is not in our anatomy or philosophy. We must strive to lift Africa to the glory of its promised and divine status.

Think . . .

"Disengagement is a response to certain demographic realities . . . Within a few years, due to the higher Arab birth rate, Jews will become a minority in the area between the Jordan River and the Mediterranean Sea. I don't want [Israel] to be South Africa because we don't believe in apartheid. We simply have to separate from the Palestinians so that we can control our own destinies."
Ehud Olmert

"Destiny provided the ladder with which Nelson Mandela rose from prison to presidency."
Anthony U. Aliche

Chapter 13

How and why does the discovery of your destiny make you a co-creator with the universal creativity?

The best and the highest thing that can happen to a man during his earthly life is to discover his assignment with destiny. This is the miracle behind the exalted works of the Twelve World Teachers, the Gnostics, the Gideons, and all who have been designated as mystics, avatars, geniuses, gurus, seers, prophets, and other highly inspired beings considered messengers of love.

A man cannot be a co-creator with the consummate universal Creator if he has not been able to discover his assignment with destiny and truth; appreciate the values of love; understand the rhythms of nature; and see things as they should be in order to be one with universal creative destiny.

It is a pity that humanity has not striven to be in tune with the Infinite, understand the power of destiny, and discover that he who cooperates with the Creator is designated as a great servant. This discovery, when actualized, brings us many benefits:

- It fosters honest and direct empowerment, which affirms David's statement that our help can come only from the Creator.

- It brings respect and recognition, inspiring people to look up to us, admire our lifestyle, and imitate those divine and rare qualities manifested in us daily when we've discovered our assignment with destiny.
- It drives us to live a purposeful life, a life determined and driven by the heavens, which makes us appreciate that God is indeed the foundation and fulcrum of destiny.
- It makes us recognize wisdom and its practical application, particularly in the originality of nature, with its consummate knowledge.
- It is the only power that will make us think universally and act with the objective principles that drive cosmic wisdom.
- It helps us be attuned to the Infinite and unified with every facet of creation.
- It helps us understand the original philosophical truths that made the great thinkers; philosophy as the occupation of the oriental wizards; and philosophy as the foundation of knowledge. With that understanding we can discover how philosophy and wisdom are the conjugal parents of knowledge. That word *conjugal*, in this context, indicates that destiny is aligned with beauty, love, light, harmony, and balance; it represents an amalgamation of knowledge.
- It makes us consider the welfare of others and act as bookkeepers within the ecosystem of universal destiny.
- It is like an electric spark illuminating our beauty and inspiring us to use it to positively affect others and put smiles on their faces.
- It helps others recognize us as geniuses and important actors in this competitive world.

Destiny makes us celebrate the glory and jubilee of Christmas; the wisdom of the apostles and their missionary achievements; the life and works of consummate geniuses like William Shakespeare, Pythagoras, Socrates, Plato, Emmanuel Kant, Mahatma Gandhi, Nelson Mandela, Spinoza, Mozart, Paracelsus, Bach, Beethoven, Walter Russell, Bill Gates, and Christopher Columbus, whose discovery was well prophesied and praised in the Book of Isaiah.

Now the handwriting on the wall is clear: the power of pen and paper are gradually attesting that A. U. Aliche, our modern Leonard Da Vinci, will soon be celebrated for cooperating with destiny to bring out his own consummate creativity.

His feat complements the extensive destined efforts of such modern greats as Rejoice C. Adiele, Queen Onyinyechi Nwokocha, and Ubani Ikemba. Aliche has enjoyed the wonderful cooperation of the environment, his friends, and his family, who have richly contributed to his destiny, which is to glorify God through his work. This is why in his prayers he always remembers the early contributions of the Russells, who saw the light of destiny in him and quickly adopted him as their destined child.

The power of destiny shines through in this statement of inspired ordination:

Oh thou God of our forefathers,

Oh thou consummate destiny to all destinies, may the glory in thee which is from the light of thy destiny employ these, my words, both spoken and unspoken, to say thank you, thou destined gift and jubilee of all eras and ages. For only in thee do we move and work; you are our power, which when harnessed opens the doors to our immortal destiny. This is the only authority that when properly employed leads us with wisdom to discover the secrets of the universe. It also empowers and inspires us to discover the marvelous secrets of harmony, balance, and unity, and the universal secrets of the one-world purpose.

The discovery of destiny makes us see the beauty of paradise, the perfection of the heavens, the mystery of the sun and moon, and the allure of the stars. When man properly harnesses and utilizes his destiny, he is honoured all over the world, adored as an immortal wealth of knowledge and inspiration, a co-creator with the universal consummate creativity. That is why this chapter concludes by asking a question, one in tune with practical rhythm of destiny:

Man, have you made an effort to discover your assignment with destiny? If you have, how have you empowered and utilized this destiny in order to be a co-creator with the authoritative ingenuity of the consummate universal creativity?

Having asked these questions, the author finally feels confident saying that destiny is the divine way of God and a unique gift for the enlightened who appreciate that our earthly purpose is to discover our destiny, put it to effective use, and apply it to the service of humanity. This is why, when death knocks at our doors, we will gladly say,

"Oh Lord, I am coming home—for thy will has been done, and thy destiny has worked wonders. I am so glad to be honoured and accepted in the paradise of the destined souls."

This is why the discovery of our destiny is the greatest thing that can happen to a human during life on earth.

In conclusion, destiny tells us to think positively in order to grow richer and to grow richer in order to save, and, as we do so, to put God at the centre of our efforts. I welcome all to discover their destiny before it is too late. When it becomes too late, earthly music will visit the mind and soul with the sad question, "Must I go empty-handed?"

Think . . .

*"If you do not create your destiny, you will have
your fate inflicted upon you."*
William Irwin Thompson

*"One cannot be a co-creator with the consummate universal
Creator if he has not been able to discover his assignment with
destiny and truth; appreciate the values of love; understand the
rhythms of nature; and see things as they should be in order to be
one with universal creative destiny."*
Anthony U. Aliche

"What can we not be when we are destiny driven?"
Anthony U. Aliche

*"The stories of great men serve as modern lessons about what
destiny can do, give, and fathom."*
Anthony U. Aliche

Chapter 14

How and why is Jesus known as the consummate star and the monument of ingenious destiny?

Among all the highly enlightened and destined Gnostics, avatars, Gideons, and mystics, including the rare class designated as geniuses, the story of Christmas, which is the most celebrated event worldwide, is considered the destined beginning of all grace. Many people do not understand the divine significance of Christmas, which is why its abuse through commercialization is commonly seen among humans. In fact, Christmas is the pinnacle of consummate destiny, the product of grace which is glorious in nature, rhythm, action, and reaction.

A work on destiny cannot exist without mentioning the monumental wisdom of the destined Christ, including how he used his destiny in becoming the son of God, the son of man, the Saviour of the whole universe, and the original mystic of the cross. His contributions to the unification of the one-world purpose have remained the destined and apostolic foundation of all universal creativity. Among the Jews, Christ remains a destined mystery, while he is a destined grace to the Gentiles. He is a gift to the universe, as revealed by Angel Gabriel to the holy mother, the Virgin Mary who was herself destined to come from the root of Abraham in order to sacrifice her son. It was all part of Jesus's glorious destiny, in accordance to the wish and mandate of his father, in order to bring salvation to the world.

Illustrating why he is a consummate star and a monument of ingenious destiny, Jesus's glorious birth heralded an unequaled jubilee, even inspiring the Eastern wise men to follow the celestial star, a sign of the destined mysticism of astrology. Empowered and enlightened by the star, they paid homage with glorious gifts, including frankincense and myrrh. But the revelation of destiny has shown that these apostles and Gnostics who visited Christ also gave gold, silver, and diamonds. Their mystical worship and adoration at Bethlehem reveal that the promise of God was gloriously fulfilled in the gift of Christ, whose destiny was to save the sinful world.

Destiny has told us that even when we are in our mother's womb, the Creator knows what we are going be. But the case of Jesus Christ remains a special one because of the extraordinary cosmic and mystical mandate by which his father in heaven enlightened him to understand his eternal assignment. He willingly submitted to the will of destiny, the wish of God's desire, and even the wish of the government during his time. At the end of the day, he trusted in the celestial power of destiny, which designated him to ask the eternal question, "Death, where is thy power?"

Furthermore, this great Messiah of all ages used the ingenuity of his destiny to heal the sick, the case of Lazarus standing tall among those miracles. The way he used the celestial current of destiny to stop the tempest, walk on water, and heal the lame and the deaf, including the woman with the flow of blood, will remain a mystery in the annals of human history and into posterity, the kingdom of destined eternity.

It is important to note that Jesus utilized the power of his destiny in speaking before the lawyers, comprised of the Pharisees and the Sadducees. The celestially inspired manner by which he won converts to his ministry, celebrated today as Christianity, was divinely fortified, something that could not have been achieved by mere intellectual prowess.

Even upon Jesus's ascension to the kingdom of his father, the monumental current of his destiny inspired the likes of John, Paul,

Matthew, and Mark to write their celebrated Gospels and epistles in memory of the consummate contribution of this destined child of the universe.

In a complex and mystical manner, author Spenser Lewis presented the achievements of Jesus Christ in his consummate edified work, *The Aquarian Gospel of Jesus the Christ*. This book would certainly make all creation understand the power of destiny, the mysticism of destiny, and the wisdom of destiny in achieving the difficult task of uniting the while world. Lewis quantifiably states that the kingdom of his father belongs to both the Jews and the Gentiles.

What an awesome human is this destined being!

His divine attributes reveal why he is from the consummate star of destiny and a monument of ingenious creativity, with a life that was focused. He reminds us that Christ holds the permanent key to unlock our destinies—or, as the scriptures state simply: *I and my father are one.*

In all creation, man was assigned the greatest task: to discern his destiny through Christ, through honest service and worship, and through the knowledge that he is the living image of God.

This book consummately presents Jesus Christ as a monumental signpost. When we behold him, we understand the meaning of the words, *Everything's gonna be alright in Christ Jesus. Everything's gonna be alright with us, with the world, with our neighbours, with our children and friends.*

To ensure that this chapter echoes the ingenuity of inspiration, it will conclude with a line from a song of destiny: "Let us with a gladsome mind praise the Lord, for he is kind, for his mercies endureth, ever faithful, ever sure." These words remind us that the greatest thing that can happen to us while we are on earth is to discover our assignment with destiny, and Jesus Christ is a destined and immortal signpost on the path to that destiny.

Think . . .

"Destiny has told us that even when we are in our mother's womb, the Creator knows what we are going be. But the case of Jesus Christ remains a special one because of the extraordinary cosmic and mystical mandate by which his father in heaven enlightened him to understand his eternal assignment. He willingly submitted to the will of destiny, the wish of God's desire, and even the wish of the government during his time. At the end of the day, he trusted in the celestial power of destiny, which designated him to ask the eternal question, 'Death, where is thy power?'"

"A work on destiny cannot exist without mentioning the monumental wisdom of the destined Christ, including how he used his destiny in becoming the son of God, the son of man, the Saviour of the whole universe, and the original mystic of the cross."

"Destiny is the living Christ in us."
Anthony U. Aliche

Chapter 15

Why did Solomon in his wisdom designate destiny as the original root of his knowledge?

Solomon was a great Gnostic, noted and cherished all over the world for becoming a student of wisdom and destiny. After realizing that he knew nothing despite his great material wealth, he discovered and designated destiny as the original source of his power, light, life, and knowledge. In a similar way, all the humans we consider immortals have acknowledged the role of destiny in their ascension to the mountaintop.

When we examine the life of Solomon, we see that he made use of destiny in several different ways:

- Destiny was his teacher.
- He honoured destiny as the root of his wisdom.
- He attributed all his achievements to the ingenuity of his destiny.
- He adopted and used destiny as his instructor, and tutor. When we read the monumental words of Solomon in the Proverbs and Song of Songs, we can see destiny's role as his life guide. His natural and spiritual message to the world includes many lessons about destiny, among them: *Seek ye destiny; love ye destiny; appreciate the power of destiny; ask the Creator to empower you with destiny; observe the laws of destiny; if you practice its teachings and precepts creation*

will call you blessed, while the angels will adore the Creator, because you are using your destiny to uplift the standard of the universe.

- He considered destiny to be both medicine and science, facilitating consummate and comprehensive scientific discoveries.
- He thought of destiny as the engineer of his soul, the designer of the rudimentary technology of his will. It was Solomon who defined and designated destiny as the supreme designer of the brotherhood of all ages, which cannot be suppressed or polluted even though prevailing challenges and circumstances may delay its manifestation.

We can achieve feats beyond greatness when we seek, ask, and knock, when we appreciate the Creator and ask Him to open our eyes in order to understand and discover our assignment with destiny. This is important, because destiny is the way to all ways, the road to all roads, the power to all powers, the ingenious light in whose love and power we see immortality.

Destiny is beyond words and above dogmas; it eschews culture and tradition; it is above religion, education, government, or any mundane power. This is why the urge to discover our destiny must be taken as a life task, a life mandate, and a life mission, one which cannot be left unaccomplished if we want to be truly in paradise. Remember that the ingenious Gnostics, avatars, and Gideons also were humans like us, but they conquered the world of earthly things, challenging the mundane in order to discover their assignment with destiny.

Many people do not understand the meaning of God's inspired words about Jesus Christ, "This is my beloved son with whom I am well pleased." From Genesis to Revelation, this is the only destined moment when God, in His own ecstasy, used this great statement. In doing so, He encourages us to know that we can be beloved sons and daughters, too, when we make an honest and diligent effort to discover our assignment with destiny.

Christopher Columbus made great discoveries through the empowered use of his destiny, as did humans like Galileo, Michael Faraday, Pythagoras, Plato, Motti, and Buddha, who was destined to tell the Eastern continents and the whole universe that the world will be a home for everyone when humans believe in and follow all tenets contained in the Sermon on the Mount.

The Sermon on the Mount is best known for the Beatitudes—and it is important in this context to define *beatitude*. In its original meaning, a beatitude was an instructional blessing, a divine law given only to the highly spiritually enlightened, the true mystics. This is why since the dawn of consciousness, the destiny of Jesus Christ drew him to the eight Beatitudes, which generally form divine law with lots of cosmic doctrines.

This chapter may have begun with a discussion of Solomon, but it is important to remember that other humans who followed the quest for the grail of knowledge were equally welcomed in the covenant of divine destiny. Here we must distinguish between destiny, whose urge is to serve in order to bring glory to the Creator, and material acquisition, which always makes one live in a fool's paradise, hampered by ego, arrogance, pomposity, the inability to be a brother's keeper, and the constant desire to be a master or a lord in order to enslave others. This is why when Solomon was enlightened to see the glory of divine destiny, he openly exclaimed to the glory of God that all acquisitions of the material world are vanity upon vanity. At the end of his time, he told his subjects to go to God in order to learn their destiny, and to use this destiny to serve and uplift humankind.

It is the purpose of this chapter to make all and sundry appreciate that the gift of destiny is for the Jews and the Gentiles, for the black and the white. Destiny remains the ingenious authority, always looking for partners and friends around the world without discrimination or favour. Simply put, destiny asks for the best of us. When we give our best, we will be inspired to appreciate that destiny is the ultimate gift from God, and we will learn to desire it, the best of the best.

Think . . .

"We in this country, in this generation, are—by destiny rather than choice—the watchmen on the walls of world freedom. We ask, therefore, that we may be worthy of our power and responsibility, that we may exercise our strength with wisdom and restraint, and that we may achieve in our time and for all time the ancient vision of 'peace on earth, good will toward men.' That must always be our goal, and the righteousness of our course must always underlie our strength. For as was written long ago: 'Except the Lord keep the city, the watchman waketh but in vain.'"
John Fitzgerald Kennedy

"Remember, people will judge you by your actions, not your intentions. You may have a heart of gold—but so does a hard-boiled egg."

"The more you are willing to accept responsibility for your actions, the more credibility you will have."
Brian Koslow

"Many fine things can be done in a day if you don't always make that day tomorrow."
Anonymous

"The fear of the Lord is the beginning of knowledge: but fools despise wisdom and instruction."
Song of Solomon

Chapter 16

What is the position of destiny in regard to our parents and upbringing?

It is important to explain that destiny, as God's immortal gift, is hereditary. It runs in the genes.

Consider how God destined Abraham to be the father of many nations, a destiny fully manifested in the life and ministry of Jesus Christ. Our parents, our biological roots, our siblings, and even our neighbours and our environment contribute greatly to our destiny, making it shine.

Parents are naturally mandated by the Creator to care for their child, even when that child is still in his mother's womb. And the Bible makes it unequivocally clear that we must honour our fathers and our mothers, and in fact anyone older than we are.

Usually, our parents are agents of nature, who uses them to ensure that our destiny shines, particularly in the following ways:

- Parents provide guidance and counseling, which is important for us to learn to toe the line.
- They are the first authority to provide us with discipline and high moral standards. Most educational experts agree that the home is a child's first classroom, and the parent his first teacher.

- They are naturally quick to direct and correct us, insisting that we do the right thing.
- Their ability to send us to a good school enhances our further educational pursuits. The Creator has always used parents to ensure that children are trained to be skillful, dynamic, and purposeful. Parents play a comprehensive role in seeing that our destiny is discovered, harnessed, and utilized.
- Parents are there to ensure that we don't become corrupt and don't associate with peers who do not understand the meaning, purpose, or mission of life. They are always there to caution us with admonitions and to correct us with the use and application of spiritual doctrine. It is the role of parents to advise us that discovering our destiny goes beyond words and thoughts.

I have had the opportunity to meet parents who are blessed with the talent of repairing broken bones and restoring their function. A look at the way the Creator bestows the gift of destiny reveals that a potter will always produce a gifted potter as a child—evidence that destiny is a thematic and positive infection that is quickly catching, because it is passed along through spiritual genetics.

Many people need to learn that destiny is determined and decided by diligence and a sense of purpose. Consider the destined leadership of some skilled statesmen in the United States, such as the Bush family. George H. W. Bush was once president of the United States, and his son worked hard to become president, as well. Their story is evidence that destiny is effective, infectious, dynamic, and purpose-driven in ensuring that natural propagation is continuous and its ingenious order is consummately adhered to. This is why a very good musician will likely have a child who will continue from where he stopped, and why, in most cases, successors have even more talent than their predecessors.

It falls within the scope of this chapter to offer several pieces of advice to parents:

- Make an honest effort to lead an objective life.

- Be spiritual, because the gift of destiny is one of the most important spiritual gifts, given through the grace of Mother Nature.
- Work to discover your own talents, destiny, and God-given gifts, for children must learn by following in their parents' footsteps.
- Strive to understand the spiritual purpose of knowing and working with the Creator, and the meaning of worship.
- Couples must always recognize the ingenious and electrifying balance between men and women.
- As role models, wives must appreciate the power of positive thinking and use the wisdom and power of prayer. They are naturally mandated to be caretakers, mothers, and prayerful wives. This is why they naturally possess psychic and spiritual qualities.
- Husbands should appreciate that God destined man to be the head of the family, to be an anchor, ensuring that his wife and family are well-protected. No matter the circumstances, a husband should never treat his wife as a slave, a babysitter, a nanny, or without regards.
- Parents must understand the value of love and the virtues of wisdom, because love and wisdom, when purposefully utilized, extol a family before the throne of the angels and before the paradise of creation. Parents must learn how to pray together, discuss together, and learn together, and how to cherish each other's values without allowing any third party to become a destructive intruder.

Lao Russell, in her ingenious and universal wisdom, stated that Third World countries are places where husbands enslave their wives. This is why civilization, evolution, and progress elude these nations, which don't understand how to discover the power and wisdom of destiny. The fact is that behind every successful man there is the immeasurable contribution of a woman, and behind every successful woman, nature has provided a man to show her the way to the mountaintop.

One of the critical laws of destiny lies with the use and application of mutual love among couples and parents.

It is safe to say that some people will be thrilled with the style and wisdom of this chapter, while others will be baffled by its tedious presentation. But the fact is that parents have a monumental role to play if their children's destiny is to shine. Therefore *when parents reject the role of destiny in their own family, they make a mockery of life, of creation, of existence, of the family circle, and of their children.*

Parents must be equal to the task that Mother Nature places upon them: to care for their children with instruction, education, guidance, and clear directives. Young people cannot be the trustees of posterity when they are not trained to harness the destiny of the future. This truth is what inspired Jesus Christ to say, "Suffer not the little children to come to me, for theirs is the kingdom of heaven." This is why God created the parental mandate, to ensure that children are well cared for—evidence that parents will work knowingly with their Creator to achieve the vision of the universal family. World peace is highly achievable through the use and application of balanced destiny, which few people have discovered as the only authority and force that shapes us in the image of the Creator.

Think . . .

"When parents reject the role of destiny in their own family, they make a mockery of life, of creation, of existence, of the family circle, and of their children."
Anthony U. Aliche

"Sometimes I ask myself what kills our childish zeal—the enthusiasm you see in growing children who, when asked, "What do you want to be when you grow up?" quickly reply, "A doctor," "A lawyer," or "A pilot." Somehow, children just know and believe that they can be what they want to be. So what happens along the way to stop them from fulfilling their childhood dreams?"
Adiele Rejoice

"Can any man be anything without destiny? No!"
Anthony U. Aliche

Chapter 17

Do the scriptures give a genealogical account of men who discovered their assignment with destiny, and how are those genealogies chronicled?

In addition to the Bible, Christianity's holy book, many other important scriptures from various religions include the stories of men and women who, inspired by the Creator, discovered their assignments with destiny. This is further evidence that a man's destiny can be fulfilled only when he decides to cooperate with the Creator.

Sadly, many people don't realize that the concept of destiny cannot be understood or explained academically—that it is a subject far beyond the scope of intellectualism.

When the Gideons were inspired to write the Bible, they included the chronicles of several immortal Gnostics who are known and defined as God's celestial symbols—Adam being first among them, followed by Noah, Moses, Joshua, Abraham, David, Elijah, Joseph, Nathaniel, Melchizedek, Elisha, Isaiah, John the Baptist, Peter, Paul, Jesus Christ, and many others.

Within the provinces of philosophy and mysticism, such great souls as Socrates, Pythagoras, Plato, Emmanuel Kant, Max Miller, Motti, St. Francis, St. Augustine, and the much-written-about Twelve

World Teachers are known worldwide as ingenious messengers of consummate destiny.

The Prophet Muhammad was destined by the Creator to found the religion now known as Islam, while all over the world, Buddhists are very faithful to the spiritual tenets and practices established by Buddha.

Lord Krishna, who was enlightened to write the sacred book known as the Bhagavad Gita, was the founder of the Krishna faith, based on the simple concept of "living and walking consciously with the wisdom of Godhead."

Divine destiny mandated and inspired Joseph Smith to establish the Church of Jesus Christ of Latter-day Saints, which contributes immeasurably to human and social development all over the world, although many people don't know much about this rather rarified religion.

Abd-ru-shin was divinely mandated and inspired to write the wonderful Grail Message, a mystical work illuminated by the light of truth. Unfortunately, because of ignorance, arrogance, and spiritual bias, humanity does not care what the Grail Message and its adherents are all about.

Spencer Lewis was destined to discover and give mankind the ancient and noble order known as Rosae Crucis. But unfortunately, because of lack of knowledge or spiritual insight into the reality of life, the uninformed have given this institution a lot of names that do not reflect the original reality of its destiny.

Manly Palmer Hall, through the wisdom of destiny, was divinely inspired to write many significant works about Oriental philosophy, mysticism, kabala, and other such topics. His factual writing about the lost continent Atlantis shows that our modern civilization is awash with ingenious discovery, which is possible only when destiny is put in focus and becomes a directive, the electrical current of the Creator.

Like Joseph Smith and his wife, Walter and Lao Russell were divinely inspired, destined to establish the University of Science and Philosophy in the American state of Virginia. Their immortal and consummate contributions in the areas of philosophy, science, engineering, technology, and medicine have remained among the greatest achievements of our contemporary civilization.

Solomon spoke eloquently about man, God, and destiny in the Book of Wisdom, especially the Song of Solomon and Ecclesiastes.

Destiny, as we know, has a lot of spiritual and scriptural backing, because it is a force that ignites us to excel and to be divinely dominated and protected at all times.

History shows us many and varied examples of the achievements of destiny, including the timeless contributions of Galileo, Albert Einstein, Michael Faraday, Christopher Columbus, William Shakespeare, Jacob Boehm, Sir Isaac Newton, Sir Isaac Pitman, Herbert Spencer, Walt Whitman, Edwin Markham, Ralph Waldo Emerson, Mark Twain, Zoroaster, and Lao Tse.

One destined person is more creative, more purposeful, more inventive, and more determined than one hundred million other people combined.

Destined humans give the world greater insight into the ingenuity of the Creator, which makes them co-creators, particularly within the sectors of education, research, commerce, industry, politics, and administration. This is why we all should strive to discover our own assignment with destiny, because any act or invention that uplifts humanity is always inspired by destiny. When Solomon asked for wisdom after having acquired vast material wealth, people didn't understand that he was asking the Creator to help him discover his assignment with destiny. When he finally discovered his destiny, the same Solomon exclaimed that all his material wealth was nothing.

We must appreciate the fact that the scriptures are the living and immortal products of destiny. This is why they are difficult to translate; any proper understanding and application of scripture must be guided by the authority of the Holy Spirit, which inspired the Gideons and the Gnostics in writing the scriptures.

To understand this chapter, whose aim is to reveal the human genealogy of destiny in world religion and philosophy, we must recognize the commonalities in the lives of these great people:

- They made God their be-all and end-all.
- They appreciated that destiny can never be given by another person or bought in the market.
- They understood that gifts of destiny are a special kind of grace which must not be compromised. That is why some of the people mentioned in this chapter sacrificed their time and even their lives for the uplifting of human dignity, and their contributions remain unique, purposeful, and immortal, although many of them are not chronicled within the annals of education. This is why I feel confident saying that destiny is like salvation: it is free to all, but the desire to have it lies in mutual, honest, respectful cooperation with the Creator. Every human being must ask God to give him his own portion of destiny, protecting him in order to put his destiny to effective work. Then we can hastily and gloriously say,

Oh thou creator of heaven and earth,
Oh thou immortal one of all ages and eras,
Oh thou embodiment of the many facets of destiny,
I bow in humility and adoration to you for bestowing upon me the gift of thy wonderful destiny.
I wish to say thank you for making me special, which is the only way I can appreciate the magnitude of the destiny you have so wonderfully and lovely bestowed upon me by your consummate destiny. You have given it to all who desire to use their destiny to uplift the standard of human life in order to serve the one-world purpose, which is dear to the Creator.

For the record, the scriptures were inspired to chronicle the accounts of humans who were blessed with divine destiny. They serve to inspire others and help them understand the biblical words, "In my father's house, there are many mansions." These mansions are the destinies we have not yet discovered, and the only way to discover them is to adore and adopt the habits of a purpose-driven life, which conforms to the laws of God, nature, and the spirit. Those who worship the Lord must worship Him in truth, love, faith, and strict obedience. Since the dawn of consciousness, the scriptures have served man as a reference point, a mystical and invaluable encyclopedia which no human has the authority to corrupt. This is nothing but the truth, and if it continues to be the truth, as it should be, it is simply God in composite and motivational destined reality.

Think . . .

"Solomon positively affected his generation with his destined wisdom."

"Destiny, as we know, has a lot of spiritual and scriptural backing, because it is a force that ignites us to excel and to be divinely dominated and protected at all times."

"Every human being must strive to ask God to give him his own portion of destiny."
Anthony U. Aliche

"And God gave Solomon wisdom and understanding exceeding much, and largeness of heart, even as the sand that is on the sea shore. And Solomon's wisdom excelled the wisdom of all the children of the east country, and all the wisdom of Egypt . . . And there came of all people to hear the wisdom of Solomon, from all kings of the earth, which had heard of his wisdom."
1Kings 4:29-30, 34

Chapter 18

Can any person discover his destiny without being in tune with the Infinite?

According to the Holy Bible, as recorded in the book of Genesis, God created the world out of nothing, but man He fashioned after His own image. Similarly, many people are born to mould their worlds out of nothingness. Those are the learned humans whom the author of this book defines and discusses as the strongholds of manifest destiny.

In the history of mankind, no person has ever created an enduring contribution without falling back on the following spiritual resources:

- the Holy Christ
- the Holy Spirit
- holy inspiration
- the Holy Trinity, the symbol of our infinite gifts

History has shown that the motto In God We Trust has served as the excelling wisdom of the American continent. The words *excelling wisdom* mean leaning on God, depending on the Holy Spirit, and valuing the wisdom of Christ. When a songwriter penned the words, "Lean on me," he revealed an understanding of the powerful language of divine inspiration.

A divinely enlightened person, like a preacher, must also embody several qualities:

- He must be honest.
- He must use wisdom in his actions and decisions.
- He must understand the truth.
- He must live a balanced life devoid of indiscipline, immoral motives, and corruption.
- He must be open-minded, living according to timeless, universal principles.
- He must be in tune with the Infinite and regularly spend time alone with God.
- His greatest desire must be to live an enlightened, objective life, fueled by the belief that knowledge is power.
- His love for philosophy must be endless, for this will empower him to think and act universally. Destiny is spiritually mystical and cosmic, holding ingenious powers to lift any human beyond rational thought.
- He must live in the world but practically and tactfully stay separate from it.
- He must embody divine virtues and destined values. He must be the picture of a real man and the practical image of God, showing humility, simplicity, humanity, and a love of service.
- He must understand the wisdom of a purpose-driven life, and he must strive to bring out the Christ inside him, which will help him realize that God's gifts are irrevocable.
- In recognizing that he is a beneficiary of God's gifts, he must strive to use those gifts to serve others without complaint or any expectation of thanks.
- He must be baptized with the wisdom of Christ, particularly that revealed in Matthew 5, in which the Sermon on the Mount offers great spiritual teachings.
- He must be a spiritual fortress, divinely endowed to contest any challenge or overcome any obstacle or temptation that would prevent him from realizing his destiny.
- He must be gentle and humble—qualities naturally favoured by destiny.

The Creator has always used wisdom to help me discover my destiny. It is the wisdom and philosophy of destiny that established the maxim, "Behind any successful man is a successful woman, and behind any failed man is an equally a failed woman."

When I received the mandate to write this book, it never occurred to me that even with my academic and intellectual prowess, the authority of enlightened inspiration would displace all the language of the academic world. I seriously believe that I will give universities a comprehensive work defining the philosophy and anatomy of destiny, a work that deserves to be included in their general curricula.

This work will help bright students discover their destiny quickly and work with it to develop practical science and technology which, when objectively used in the pursuit of destiny, will help the universal world through the development of a permanent, structured system of engineering.

In order to achieve this feat, it is important to note that no human being is capable of discovering his destiny without being in tune with the infinite—the anatomy, authority, wisdom, knowledge, and electrifying foundation of enlightened and ingenious destiny.

The time has come for humans to establish an organization of destined people displaying the characteristics of destined souls. When Mrs. Walter Russell was divinely inspired to establish the Intelligent Age of Character Club, she knew that very few people ever discover their assignment with destiny.

The Infinite is the giver of life and knowledge, the authority of wisdom, and the giver of all destinies. This is why the works of destined people are visible in inventions, technology, philosophy, engineering, science, industry, service, administration, politics, and other important areas of our lives.

We can see various case studies of people who used their political destiny to serve and uplift their nations, among them Nelson Mandela, who rose from prison to presidency; Guatama Buddha, who was central to the liberation and independence of India; and George Washington, whose immortal contributions inspired Americans to establish their capital of Washington DC, with its famed White House. Their works, all accomplished despite a high level of challenge, reveal that destiny is all-encompassing, all-embracing, and all-involving. But no man can discover his true assignment with destiny without depending on the power and directives of the Infinite.

Given the force of destiny, it can serve to make us titanic trailblazers. It is the spiritual power behind our success. And when we properly harness it, we can then use our destiny to help others discover their own destiny. But that is possible only when man is aligned with God's will, practicing nothing less than mutual and perfect cooperation with the do's and don'ts of the Infinite, the immortal laws that make our destiny unfold.

This is why destiny is the only force that answers the call to service, the urge for divine light, the quest for consummate love, and the mandate to be our brother's keeper and sister's lover.

For the record, destiny is the ingenious coming together of all human and spiritual achievement, which is impossible if man is not in total agreement and cooperation with the Infinite Intelligence.

Think . . .

"For those whom God to ruin has designed,
He fits for fate, and first destroys their mind."
John Dryden

"One God, one law, one element,
And one far-off divine event,
To which the whole creation moves."
Alfred Tennyson

"God created the world out of nothing, but man He fashioned
after His own image; many are born to mould their worlds out of
nothingness."
Mike Omoloye

"The motto In God We Trust has served as the excelling wisdom
of the American continent. The words 'excelling wisdom' mean
leaning on God."
Anthony U. Aliche

"How do geese know when to fly to the sun? Who tells them the
seasons? How do we humans know when it is time to move on? As
with the migrant birds, so surely with us, there is a voice within, if
only we would listen to it, that tells us certainly when to go forth
into the unknown."
Elisabeth Kubler-Ross

"Destiny is infectious when you desire to discover your
assignment with her."
Anthony U. Aliche

Chapter 19

Why is destiny defined as the spiritual strength of our success?

Success is never possible if our destiny is not put into effective action. Unfortunately, many people do not understand or appreciate what purpose-driven success is all about.

When we consider the path, the wisdom, the strength, and the power that lead to true success, we can appreciate that with the use and application of our destiny, success is assured, its protection guaranteed, and its consolidation perfected. This is why Solomon, at the pinnacle of his success, praised God as its foundation.

Solomon, the wisest man who ever lived because of his intellectual and spiritual acumen, had at this point decided to put aside considerations of money and material things and the urges and lures of the flesh, because he knew everything of the flesh is vanity upon vanity.

Destiny is defined as the spiritual strength and power of our success for several reasons:

- Destiny, by its design, is success-driven.
- Destiny is spiritually empowered.
- Destiny is God in action, realized when man is in absolute accord with God's directives.

- Destiny is the practical use of divine wisdom to create lasting success.
- Destiny is the eternal current that makes us know that God is the foundation of the living word.
- Success, as the way of the blessed, cannot be achieved without destiny in action.
- Destiny, as an irrevocable gift from God, cannot be realized without the spiritual strength of the Creator, who is through destiny eternalized and galvanized as grace in action.
- The use of destiny guarantees honest success, which comes naturally without hurting anyone, without destruction, without corruption, without lies, and without disobedience to natural laws. The lives of Christ, Buddha, Muhammad, and Plato, for example, remain timeless lessons for us all, because they used destiny to discover the honest and balanced wisdom of the Creator.

For these reasons, we will continue to respect, remark upon, enjoy, and bless their successes into posterity.

The only authority that can explain true success—its origin, power, purpose, and service to humanity—is destiny. Through destiny, we can understand why God's yoke does not hurt.

Since the dawn of consciousness, destiny has been the way of the enlightened. It drove the power and love of life of the blessed angels and the wisdom of the apostolic foundation, which gave birth to philosophy and perfect wisdom.

A look at the many manifestations of destiny shows that we can use its authority and consummate wisdom to make great achievements: to reach the heavens; to attain grace; to become kings, heroes, or presidents. Destiny is like a monumental magnet that naturally draws people to you. Just like the balanced law of homogeneity.

There is a question that we must ask ourselves: *What can we achieve if destiny does not guide our path?* After all, even the most intelligent people can become failures; the most astute managers, working in the wrong field, can become "mis-managers."

When we are aligned with all facets of our destiny, with its varying rhythms and rhymes, we find that stress, pain, want, and spiritual failure become things of the past.

It is important to remember that poverty—on an individual, familial, communal, societal, national, or continental level—will remain personal and acute when those affected do not make an honest effort to discover their assignments with destiny. This is the difference between the white race and black race. Every effort of the white race is geared toward discovering the technology of their destiny, the scientific engineering of their destiny, and the philosophy and the metaphysics of their destiny, and this is why they are always investigating the unseen. Meanwhile the black race is always using the byproducts of those discoveries, which because they are based upon the unseen are labeled by the uninformed as cultism or the occult.

When properly harnessed, destiny yields miraculous results; it is comparable to the right drug prescribed for sickness after proper testing and analysis.

Our spiritual strength guarantees the practical utilization of our physical strength. Destiny admonishes us to use our spiritual strength in the following ways:

- Be an effective planner with dynamic execution.
- Strive to be alone with God. This facilitates the functioning of destiny, which in turn ignites the spark of purpose-driven success in our lives.
- Be practical, not theoretical.
- Be positive no matter the circumstances, difficulties, or challenges.
- Be careful, be prayerful, and creatively involve yourself in practical and objective communion with the Creator. We

derive the most spiritual strength when we are most in union with our soul.

- Destiny wants us to bring out our Christ-like instincts, which will in turn strengthen our spiritual powers for the attainment of enlightenment, a purpose-driven life, and honest service to others, in synchronicity with the principles of the brotherhood of man.
- Success that is not deeply rooted in the supernatural power and strength of destiny is comparable to a mighty empire built on a mountaintop—it can be blown away by the slightest storm.

Have You Discovered Your Assignment with Destiny? is all about discovering and successfully using your gifts, harnessing your power in order to be a co-creator with the Infinite dimension, destiny. At any point in time, our success speaks volumes about God's grace, His glory, and His love, and about our desire. He who discovers his destiny is like a man who has found a good wife.

We must learn to appreciate that the spiritual strength behind our success is only guaranteed when we put God first. That is why the destiny of America has remained one of the glorious stories of creation, ever since the destined explorer Christopher Columbus discovered the New World, which became a home where everyone wants to belong, and where new inventions still shape the destiny of every child. The reasons for this country's achievements greatly lie in its motto, In God We Trust, a written reflection of dynamic spiritual strength.

Think . . .

"The use of destiny guarantees honest success, which comes naturally without hurting anyone, without destruction, without corruption, without lies, and without disobedience to natural laws."

"We must learn to appreciate that the spiritual strength behind our success is only guaranteed when we put God first."
Anthony U. Aliche

"Tempt not the stars, young man, Thou canst not play with the severity of fate."
John Ford

"The whole secret of a successful life is to find out what it is one's destiny to do, and then do it."
Henry Ford

Chapter 20

How can you affect others in order to help them discover their assignment with destiny?

In the immortal words of the enlightened thinker Dr. Walter Russell, as he wrote in his wonderful work *The Book of Beauty from The Message of the Divine Iliad*:

> *"He whose inner ears heareth My voice in falling waters—in soft breezes of hillside pines—in tempestuous tornado and rhythms of pounding sea—in the motion of star systems of My firmament, in the silences of interchanging lights and shadows interplaying o'er hill and dale-or in the moods of the winds and the light of earth's moon, yea, he who is so attuned to Me is already in My house and createth with Me.*
>
> *"To him I give all-knowing and all-power to think My universe into rhythmic, balanced forms with Me.*
>
> *"To these who are thus illumined by My Light I speak in rhythms of Light for the uplift of other men. Such illumined ones are My messengers who re-inspire other men and open for them the doors to My kingdom."*

The monumental wisdom of this text reveals that no human being is capable of changing the life of another if that human is not purposefully using his own destiny. Such a human must be a co-creator, a great messenger of truth and love, an enlightened universal thinker who is cosmically driven because he has discovered his assignment with destiny. He is serving his destiny with the power of the Creator, daily translating that power into the different facets and creations of destiny. It is at this point that such a human can spontaneously and freely say, "Come, let us work for the Creator. Come and follow me." These were the immortal words of Jesus when he discovered his own assignment with destiny, one that we celebrate daily as the sacrament and jubilee of the victory on the cross.

When you are honest in all your claims and actions; when, by putting smiles on their faces, you ensure that people appreciate the Creator, particularly at a time of suffering and tempests; when all hopes are gone; when it seems as if the whole world has condemned you with abject neglect—then you discover that destiny, like a whirlwind, is always using someone to put a smile on a sorrowful face, to make people appreciate that love is the divine and truth of God.

There are several ways you can use your discovered destiny to positively affect the lives of other people:

- You can render them honest service.
- You can educate them through the use and application of destiny.
- You can empower them by helping them free themselves from poverty.
- You can teach them to believe in themselves and God.
- You can care for them with the use and application of your destiny, which is a special gift from God.
- You can teach them the skills to discover their own destiny, which is as good as making them fishermen rather than just fish eaters.
- You can establish an educational centre, an industrial incubator, or a research bank, or you can use the might of your destiny to start a community of small—and medium-scale farmers, industrialists, artists, and craftsmen.

- Destiny, by its nature, does not allow people to act and react negatively, but because of the power of its wisdom, it helps us to be real humans, making us active and positive. This is why a detailed reading of this book, especially this chapter on helping others discover their destiny, will inspire a teaching instinct and desire in someone who is close to discovering his own destiny. This is why the works and discoveries of such geniuses as Shakespeare, Beethoven, Paracelsus, Mozart, Christopher Columbus, Michael Faraday, and the mystic who wrote the Bhagavad-gita remain the foundation of a good education. Universities and academic organizations continue to include the immortal works of these great thinkers in their contemporary curricula.

The spiritual circles of the destiny of mystics like Jesus Christ, the Prophet Muhammad, Buddha, and Lord Krishna were created to influence the secular and spiritual world. These great Gnostics used their destinies to positively contribute to world culture and mankind's traditions, norms, education, philosophy, religion, theology, metaphysics, and theosophy. Destiny is always in search of honest messengers who can use its boundless wisdom to affect others positively so that they will believe that our assignment with destiny is the basis of honest living.

One of the goals of this book is to recommend that an exploration of destiny be part of any academic curriculum. That is because destiny is the only authority that can help us discover the dormant genius inside us, the genius that will help us cast aside and destroy mediocrity. It is an authoritative foundation that we can use to learn the secrets of science and technology, which we can use, in turn, to learn the sacred teachings of all ages. That is why an ingenious discovery inspired by deep thought about destiny is always used to affect people's lives positively and progressively, and that's why he who rejects or neglects his assignment with destiny has an eternal case with Mother Nature, a case that will follow him as a monumental stigma. The urge to discover your destiny must be purpose-driven; you must use its gifts, power, knowledge, health, and wisdom to positively and significantly affect the lives of human beings. After someone has discovered his assignment with destiny, every day is purposefully determined, characterized by service to humanity. The use of this power creates further blessings. Many mere humans regard these blessings as miracles, and those bequeathed with these powers as miracle-workers.

Using our destiny to affect the lives of others positively and meaningfully is the only way we can say thank you to God for making us special. The question millions of readers must answer is, *Am I using my destiny to thank God?*

Think . . .

"No human being is capable of changing the life of another if that human is not purposefully using his own destiny."

"You can affect others by establishing an educational centre, an industrial incubator, or a research bank, or you can use the might of your destiny to start a community of small- and medium-scale farmers, industrialists, artists, and craftsmen."

"Teaching people to use and apply inspiration in their business is another way of saying thank you to the Creator, who destined you to be a teacher."
Anthony U. Aliche

Chapter 21

Why is destiny known as the original root, resource, and power of the secrets of light?

It is important to address this subject using wisdom that is rooted firmly in the truth. Many people do not know that destiny is the authority of consummate light, consummate wisdom, and objective knowledge, focusing on the ideal in love, light, success, and the other positive elements of life.

The secrets of light represent great knowledge which can be discovered only when we strive to ignite our destiny. But we must begin by discovering the purpose of our origin and the meaning, wisdom, and origin of our roots. We must equally understand the powers of our roots, for only in this wisdom can we understand the knowledge, root, and philosophy of destiny. We can measure the secrets of light only if we are able to measure the wisdom of destiny.

When someone strives to discover the secrets of light inside him, he does not need a physician to tell him that he has discovered the secrets of destiny. The change is immediately apparent: suddenly he acts universally and thinks cosmically, and the light in destiny sharpens his sense of understanding.

Again, destiny is God in action, occurring when man is in dynamic and absolute cooperation with his Creator. Given the power of destiny, therefore, we are able to have and create great things, including the following:

❖ enormous resources with abundant wealth
❖ generosity with the drive to serve humanity
❖ balanced wisdom and the gift of using it to uplift humanity
❖ the ability to think deeply about truth and love
❖ the wisdom to distinguish between people who uplift us and those who don't
❖ the gift of being loved and the ability to show love, kindness, and understanding, and to appreciate the problems of others
❖ the natural inclination to act rightly and positively and to place others before ourselves
❖ the love, respect, and understanding of others, and the ability to generate universal love beyond words and thoughts.

No man can know himself, the Creator, the universe, and the secrets of light without first discovering his assignment with destiny. This is the honest and balanced power that extols the immeasurable virtues of the Twelve World Teachers, the few geniuses the world has had since the dawn of consciousness, the great prophets and seers, the enlightened mystics, the Gnostics, and the Gideons. The science of destiny and its technology foster the creation of permanent ideas, great assets, and monumental wonders that often seem like mysteries to those who have not discovered their assignment with destiny.

As Walter Russell told us, he who discovers his assignment with destiny is a great scholar, a great giant, a great mystic, becoming one of the original roots of wisdom.

Our friend, an apostle of destiny named Mike Omoleye, has unequivocally stated that "destiny is the power to all powers and force to all forces." When it is properly harnessed and used, therefore, it leads to the wisdom of mystical realization, the secrets of light, and the secrets of secrets. Or as the author of this book concludes, "Destiny is the authority to lift ourselves up, the power to light others up, the wisdom to understand the secrets of light, and the philosophy to appreciate the true meaning of life." The author also opines that no man can create an enduring act without first discovering the secrets of light contained in his destiny, for self-discovery is the honest route to self-actualization, self-fulfillment, and self-realization.

Renowned psychologist Helen Anselm powerfully describes destiny as "the only light whose speed is more monumental than the speed of the angels and the only authority which we can use to discover the secrets of knowledge." She concludes that the use and application of destiny makes one ennobled, cared for, and sought after.

As we consider the wonders of the secrets of light, we must appreciate the fact that without discovering our assignment with destiny, we simply wallow about without purpose or direction, as if we were in a labyrinth. But with the power and the secrets of light, which are manifestations of the wisdom of destiny, we become co-creators with the universal Creator and co-thinkers with the universal Thinker.

I hereby offer these words for use now and into posterity: *No man is capable of creating an enduring act without discovering his assignment with destiny and appreciating the secrets of the wisdom of light.* Only in knowledge and light can man live a fulfilled and meaningful life. The secrets of light comprise our greatest assignment, which must surely ignite the original roots of our destiny.

Think . . .

"No man is capable of creating an enduring act without discovering his assignment with destiny and appreciating the secrets of the wisdom of light."
Anthony U. Aliche

Chapter 22

Why is destiny known as a mission that must be fulfilled through honest accomplishments?

It is important to explain that destiny is a spiritual mission and vision, a mystical goal which must be accomplished. The Creator, who works daily with destiny and wisdom, has given us the task of discovering our assignment with destiny and employing the authoritative ingenuity of destiny to serve the world honestly, to impact knowledge, to educate others, and to improve our own wisdom. This is why many schools of thought define destiny as a cosmic mission to be fulfilled.

Few people truly know what destiny is. I define destiny as the power of the North Star, the power of Christmas, the miraculous power that comes from above. So destiny, when we discover our assignment with it, certainly will extol the divine virtues, which are freely bestowed upon us.

Destiny is a mission we all must fulfill, a life we all must live, a price we all must pay. It is a task, a spiritual assignment, which everyone must participate in. Destiny holds the key to our success, empowerment, enlightenment, understanding, knowledge, and wisdom, and it starts to manifest itself as soon as our parents name and pray for us. Destiny blesses us through the word of God, directs us in the wisdom of Christ, and guides us to be noble souls. The ministry and mission of destiny are what made Christ the victor of the cross rather than the loser of Gethsemane.

Christ's ministry and mission—ensuring that the grave could not hold the key with which he unlocked the secrets of destiny—is a glorious challenge. It is a clarion call to all and sundry to work in the pattern of destiny, to partake in its ministry and mission of destiny, and to understand its meaning so that we can appreciate the wisdom of walking with destiny. That is why this chapter appears at the centre of our discussion of spiritual awakening.

Not only have very few people fulfilled their assignment with destiny, but very many people appear to be alienated from the ministry and mission of destiny. The power of destiny means nothing to such people; they dismiss the wisdom of destiny with a wave of their hand; the knowledge and vision of destiny make no impact on their small minds.

Christopher Columbus considered his assignment to be a task, a ministry, a mission, and a vision that had to be accomplished. He tackled this task with faith in God, with hope in Christ, and the inspired ingenuity that was a business necessity. The land known today as America started with Columbus's destiny: discovering a New World.

Praise be to God who has made us know that destiny is a mission that must be fulfilled, a vision that must be followed, a ministry that can grow only when we adhere to the truth, walk knowingly with the Creator, and understand that life has no meaning when we do not know our destiny. This is why and how destiny must be the key to our success strategies.

When we accomplish the mission of destiny, we can do the following:

- live an abundant, honest life
- live in the light of truth
- discover the secrets of success

- discover the secrets of love
- enlighten our lives with divine illumination
- walk in wisdom with absolute conviction
- live a visionary life characterized by honest and fulfilling accomplishments
- conquer poverty and replace it with plenty
- stand tall and proclaim that God is the father and fulcrum of destiny.

The discovery of destiny leads to all gates, all roots, and all paths. The fulfillment of destiny at any point in time leads to heaven on earth, with success in strategy, and abundance.

Not only this, but destiny is our spiritual heritage and natural birthright, the way of the faithful and the highly enlightened. Its discovery brings permanent joy, perfect exhilaration, consummate knowledge, and great wisdom. Consider these stories of destined people:

- Jesus fulfilled his mission with destiny, and as a result we enjoy and celebrate the monumental feast of our Saviour, Jesus.
- Christopher Columbus fulfilled his assignment, and today virtually everyone wants to live in America, which he named "the New World."
- Michael Faraday accomplished his mission with destiny, and today the worlds of science, technology, engineering, industry, commerce, economics, and education use electricity in glorious celebration of his immortal works.
- Mungo Park was a central figure in the discovery of the river Niger, and today we celebrate and enjoy his victories.
- John Dalton, a gifted and enlightened scientist, developed an atomic theory which has stood the test of time, particularly in the fields of chemistry and physics. Today Dalton's atomic theory and principles have been fully incorporated into the teaching of chemistry.

- Dr. Walter Russell discovered and fulfilled his assignment with destiny, and today he is considered by many to be the American Leonardo da Vinci.

A lot of people do not know that our assignment with destiny must be discovered, must be taken seriously, must be fulfilled in a practical way. When destiny is at work, so is God. The time has come for each of us to discover, understand, and appreciate our assignment with destiny so that every facet of our lives is tailored toward fulfilling that assignment.

For the record, he who discovers his destiny makes a mission and then fulfills the mandate of that mission. He is more than a genius; he is like a fulfilled mystic. The power, wisdom, resources, and knowledge of destiny, when put to use properly and effectively, return blessings more dazzling than jewels and more valuable than diamonds or gold. We all are mandated to make destiny our mission and to use the power and glory of Christ to fulfill this mission, which is destiny in action. The greatest blessing we can receive on earth is to discover our assignment with destiny and use its power to live fruitfully. We are mandated through our destiny to establish monuments and achieve a mission, and that is why destiny is defined as God in action when man is in practical cooperation with him.

Think . . .

"Destiny is a spiritual mission and vision, a mystical goal which must be accomplished. The Creator, who works daily with destiny and wisdom, has given us the task of discovering our assignment with destiny."

"Michael Faraday accomplished his mission with destiny, and today the worlds of science, technology, engineering, industry, commerce, economics, and education, use electricity in glorious celebration of his immortal works."

"A lot of people do not know that our assignment with destiny must be discovered, must be taken seriously, must be fulfilled in a practical way."
Anthony U. Aliche

"I seldom end up where I wanted to go, but almost always end up where I need to be."
Douglas Adams

Chapter 23

What can constitute delays in the actualization of our destiny?

Delay at any point in time does not mean denial; it does not mean stoppage, nor does it mean outright destruction.

A lot of people feel sick, discouraged, and unwilling to move forward when a challenge comes their way; they don't realize that a challenge can be a catalyst to success. It provides us with a ladder with which we can climb from problems to praise.

Testimony to this revelation is Jesus Christ, who became the triumphant Son of God and the victorious Son of man because he was compelled by the challenges of the Pharisees and Sadducees of his era. These hypocrites served as a catalyst to the divine consummation of the destiny of Jesus.

Many other biblical figures were able to turn delays into the victorious actualization of their destinies. Among them were Joshua, David, Moses, Abraham, Noah, Elijah, Elisha, John the Baptist, and Melchizedek.

Keep them in mind when you consider the following factors that can cause delays in actualizing our desired destiny:

- our family circle with its tumultuous challenges

- our current environment with its chaos and problems
- our biological roots with their multifarious challenges
- our friends and family, who through deceitful acts may impede our harmonious actualization of our destiny
- some religious practices, whose baseless rules and restrictions must be forgotten
- the lack of an education that would enhance the power our destiny by teaching us how to use it
- societal challenges stemming from arbitrary mores and cultural traditions
- natural factors like poverty, illness, and bad luck.

Many women and men have been prevented from actualizing their destiny because of circumstances beyond their control. I invite those people to work with the philosophy of the winning destiny, with its ingenious and illumined wisdom.

There is an English saying, "Tell me who your friends are and I will tell you who you are." The meaning of this adage is very clear in this context. A lot of people have turned bad because of bad company and bad friends. Therefore who your friends are has a lot to do with the actualization of your destiny.

Other factors that can delay actualization include

- a lack of vision
- a lack of foresight
- a lack of wisdom
- a lack of knowledge with understanding
- a lack of courage
- a lack of determination.

We must turn to God, who can help us overcome the factors that block our progress and the actualization of our destiny.

A noted songwriter once said that he had no power of his own; simply invited Jesus Christ to bring his destiny, wisdom, and courage, as well as the power of the cross, to empower him to actualize his destiny. He knew full well that destiny cannot be actualized if God is not in absolute control.

While every disappointment is a blessing in disguise, we also must work hard to forestall future disappointments—and to do that, we must be practical and dynamic. A look at what constitutes a winning destiny with its enlightened wisdom reveals that we must be courageous and determined; we must be willing to see challenge as a way forward.

To actualize our destiny, we must develop the courage to appreciate ourselves as a living image of God and to understand the power of our neighbours.

Destiny is interested in working only with courageous, tireless, and fearless humans; that's why a great destiny actualized always correlates with an objective life.

An objective life is a life of future and vision; a life of destiny; a life of wisdom and practical knowledge; a life of asking God to take the lead so we might follow; a life of saying, "I will not die because my redeemer lives"; a practical life of converting poverty into plenty, plenty into perfection, perfection into purity, purity into eternity, eternity into vision, vision into light, and light into God's destined realization.

This state of living brings us into accord with the goodness of the angels; with the beauty and power of the saints; and with the winning destiny and power of Jesus Christ. Thus saved, we are loved rather than hated; cared for rather than neglected; accepted rather than rejected; and creative rather than destructive. The actualization of our destiny lies in our cooperation with God; when He delays your destiny, He should be considered your teacher and your friend.

Let it be established that anyone who purposely delays your destiny is only giving the Creator a reason to respond. So the consequences will come back to him as karma. They will return like a boomerang, affecting his family even into the next generation—evidence that no man can deny, delay, or destroy your destiny, which is your assignment with the Creator.

In actualizing our destiny we must be careful, courageous, tactful, secretive, and prayerful, ensuring that we use the wisdom of winning destiny to protect ourselves and prevent our enemies from knowing our secrets. One of the cardinal and immortal laws of destiny is the same as the spiritual law of success: he who discovers his assignment with destiny must work in the light of truth in order to protect, preserve, and safeguard the consummate wealth and resources of destiny. This is the truth that we must remember in order to avoid delay in the actualization of our destiny. Because destiny is a mission that must be accomplished, a garden that must be watered every day. And as our predecessors have done it honestly and rightly, we can, with the wisdom and courage of God, do it even better than they.

For the record, this chapter serves well as a sermon promoting the wonders of destiny.

Think . . .

"A lot of people feel sick, discouraged, and unwilling to move forward when a challenge comes their way; they don't realize that a challenge can be a catalyst to success. It provides us with a ladder with which we can climb from problems to praise."
Anthony U. Aliche

"I have no regrets in my life. I think that everything happens to you for a reason. The hard times that you go through build character, making you a much stronger person."
Rita Mero

"I can't control my destiny, I trust my soul, my only goal is just to be. There's only now, there's only here. Give in to love or live in fear. No other path, no other way. No day but today."
Jonathan Larson

"It's choice—not chance—that determines your destiny."
Jean Nidetch

"Out of our beliefs are born deeds; out of our deeds we form habits; out of our habits grows our character; and on our character we build our destiny."
Henry Hancock

"Whatever course you decide upon, there is always someone to tell you that you are wrong. There are always difficulties arising which tempt you to believe that your critics are right. To map out a course of action and follow it to an end requires courage."
Ralph Waldo Emerson

Chapter 24

What are the main lessons to be learned from these delays when they occur?

Delays are typically considered bothersome or even dangerous. But it is also true that delays—whether they result from a natural event or a man-made one, such as our own bad attitude or problems within our family circle—can serve as great catalysts in the unfolding of our destiny.

This goes to show that no man can put God to the test, no man can challenge God, and no other authority can fathom the course of your destiny. Hence any act of delay shows that God is at work for the better unfolding of your destiny.

There are some lessons to be learned about delays:

- Delays should make us be more careful.
- They should cause us to appreciate the fact that prevention is better than cure.
- They should empower us to be positive in our thoughts and actions.
- They should remind us to be purpose-driven at all times, simply because destiny, properly harnessed, makes us stand tall above our contemporaries, above the intellectuals and academicians. Destiny, when discovered, makes us living and consummate authorities.

- One of the greatest lessons we must remember boils down to keeping to ourselves, listening with the ears of destiny, partnering with the secrets of destiny, and ensuring that our great ideas are not dashed to the ground.
- Through these delays, we also increase our faith, learning to trust God before any man.
- Destiny has an obvious nature and rhythm. Those who pay attention to them and discover their assignment with destiny live a simple life characterized by humility, politeness, and charity. The onus lies upon them to never be wicked, to remain ever religious, and to never compete. Simply discovering their assignment with destiny makes them lords.
- Another supreme lesson, one that has transcended the ages, is that these delays bring us closer to God. They put us in tune with the Infinite and with nature, empowering us to recognize the capriciousness of man.
- In one of my books, *Great Maxims for the Contemporary Era,* I state that man's disappointment begins God's appointment, and that man's delay—no matter the wait or the reason—extols destiny as the powerful consummation of God's gifts.

Many people are crude, others are wicked, and still others are uncharitable. But we must keep in mind that life and nature are intertwined. Like a boomerang, what you give to others comes back to you—and what you receive is often far more than you gave.

Destiny discovered is powerful, returning numerous gifts which can salvage people's lives, freeing them from ridicule and abject poverty. When we celebrate the destiny of Jesus Christ, it goes to show that the concerted efforts of the Pharisees, the Sadducees, Pontius Pilate, and even his fellow Jews could not keep this great man from discovering and achieving his assignment with destiny.

One of the greatest lessons we learn from delays is to appreciate the wisdom and philosophy of simply watching and praying, as mandated by Christ. Delays make us love everybody but trust a few, and they remind us that we should never entrust someone else with our valuables or responsibilities, because man is naturally mischievous and wicked. This is why any human striving to discover his assignment with destiny learns to lean permanently on the Creator.

Consider what is happening to American entrepreneur Bill Gates, who has become wary of others because his genius in computers and information technology has earned him monumental wealth, which has attracted great envy and jealousy. As a result, he has decided to leave his wealth to mankind through a charitable organization, the Bill Gates Foundation.

Part of the purpose of this chapter, therefore, is to serve as an admonishment that we should be very careful when we discover our assignment with destiny; that we should live as examples for those who are still striving to discover their assignment with destiny; and that we should be careful of where we go and what we do, because the world is full of evil, jealousy, envy, hatred, and apathy.

This is why, as Lao Russell tells us, *you are accountable to the Creator if you do not work assiduously to protect and preserve your reputation. Your destiny, discovered, will be a celebration of success, achievements, and accomplishments.*

This is why when a challenge comes your way—and particularly when you must discover your assignment with destiny—you have to be careful and prayerful. If you don't, you may need a higher authority to tell you that you are vulnerable to attack.

It is important to understand that as we strive to discover our assignment with destiny, every lesson that comes our way should be accepted as a constant, another step toward conquest and adventure. If you are being envied and attacked without reason, remember that in every situation, you are alone with God.

Do not fail to bless those who challenge you and to appreciate the fact that challenge is a catalyst to success. After you discover your assignment with destiny, work to propagate your success, and use any wealth derived from your destiny to put smiles on people's faces, whether or not they thank you. When you are forced to learn life's lessons the hard way, know that you are blessed, because you're being trained to conquer bigger challenges, reach greater heights, and advance further. So never give up, never doubt your ability, and never forget that the enlightened presence of the living God is always around you. All these admonitions and lessons are ladders of truth; use them to advance to further victories. Always remember that success comes from God while victory belongs to man, and the combination of success and victory makes us appreciate that destiny can only be discovered when we open ourselves to God's anointing. This requires us to have an in-depth understanding of His divine actions, which are naturally driven by wisdom, grace, blessings, and fruitfulness. Never forget to tell God thank you for the lessons of life.

Think . . .

"No man can challenge God, and no other authority can fathom the course of your destiny. Hence any act of delay shows that God is at work for the better unfolding of your destiny."
Anthony U. Aliche

"Ideas are like stars; you will not succeed in touching them with your hands. But like the seafaring man on the desert of waters, you choose them as your guides, and following them you will reach your destiny."
Carl Schurz

"Fate leads the willing and drags along the unwilling."
Seneca

"Destiny: a tyrant's authority for crime and a fool's excuse for failure."
Ambrose Bierce

"Take time to deliberate; but when the time for action arrives, stop thinking and go in."
Napoleon Bonaparte

Chapter 25

Can the success of one's destiny be celebrated—and, if so, how and why?

All over the world, people celebrate the holy birth of Jesus Christ, his consummate victory at the cross, and his glorious ascension to heaven. The way he single-handedly took death from the hands of Lucifer has remained the greatest joy of all creation.

People celebrate their birthdays even though they have achieved nothing and have not discovered their assignment with destiny. Such celebrations have become social events, part of popular culture and tradition.

It is important to explain that one's destiny needs to be celebrated. It needs to be upheld as a way to say thank you to the Almighty Creator, to the Holy Spirit, to inspiration, to the guiding angels, and to Jesus Christ, who is central to the consummate celebration of destiny.

A look at the immortal contributions of the Twelve World Teachers, who gave the world its founding culture, traditions, wisdom, philosophy, education, religion, and inventions, reveals that in Asian countries, spiritual leaders like Buddha, the Prophet Muhammad, Lao Tse, Lord Krishna, and Akhenaten are routinely celebrated.

In the Western world, we celebrate the immortal contributions of Jesus Christ, Plato, Paracellus, Beethoven, Bash, and others. The way we celebrate Christmas, our culture's greatest tradition, is an eloquent testimony to the fact that the successful discovery of one's destiny is worth being celebrated, honoured, and discussed in order to say, "Oh God and Father, you are mightier than any weapon."

In Nigeria, for instance, we celebrate the destiny of our liberation from abhorrent colonial rule. The same sort of celebration takes place in Ghana, Mozambique, Kenya, South Africa, and other countries around the world. These celebrations fulfill a prophecy in the Book of Isaiah, which also predicted the discovery of the New World by the destined Christopher Columbus.

When the Isaiah, now known as a monumental Gnostic, made this prophecy, people were not civilized enough to appreciate that God was talking to them through the mouth of a holy prophet. Even today, although America is acknowledged as the country where everyone wants to live, the world does not celebrate the prophetic prophecy of Isaiah or the great accomplishment of Christopher Columbus.

Indians traditionally celebrate the immortal contributions of Buddha, Gandhi, and Krishna. The immortal victory of the Philippians' Aquinas is celebrated all over the world, and in Africa the great Liberian leader Salif stands as evidence that destiny at any point in time needs to be celebrated.

Celebrating your destiny does not call for drinking, smoking, and other such merriment; instead it calls for deep reflection, deep appreciation, and great honour and service to the Creator, and it calls for a lot of prayers and thanksgiving to the founder and fountain of destiny.

Unfortunately, man does not understand that he cannot discover his assignment with destiny without the Creator.

Across the world there are those whose achievements are worthy of being celebrated. Among them is Nostradamus, whose predictions and prophecies made him famous worldwide as a seer of truth. In Greece, people celebrate the wonderful and consummate achievements of Plato, Pythagoras, and Socrates. In Great Britain, people offer prayers at the permanent resting place of William Shakespeare, the icon of literary ingenuity.

When we celebrate the success of people's destiny, we are only asking the heavens for more knowledge, more strength, more wisdom, more achievement, and greater accomplishments. In the future we will celebrate our creative successes with a museum of knowledge which will show into posterity that all our blessings come from God.

It is not a sin to celebrate the success of one's destiny or even to assemble a committee of great thinkers to celebrate the achievements of one's destiny. Rather, this provides a platform for teaching younger people that life is not static, that life can be marked by great success, and that destiny belongs to all, particularly those who set their sights high.

When we celebrate the success of one's destiny, it goes a long way to provoke the heavens into doing and giving more. This is why people routinely gather together to praise and honour God—particularly those who have been privileged to discover their assignment with destiny.

The power of destiny has always been mightier than academic excellence, bigger than material wealth, and more valuable than gold and diamonds. Every day of our life, we must celebrate the ultimate manifestation of destiny: the success of Jesus Christ, the victory of his birth, and the power and glory that make him the Son of God and the Son of man.

Within the realm of inventors, we celebrate the consummate achievements of Michael Faraday, Isaac Newton, Isaac Pitman, and

Thomas Edison, and within the area of mathematical engineering we celebrate and remember Pythagoras, H. A. Clement, L. A. Durrell etc.

The monumental nature of these men's achievements—all functions of destiny—reveal why we should celebrate them: because so many men have lived their lives without discovering their assignment with destiny, while others have strived but failed to do. When we discover our assignment with destiny, we should celebrate in order to thank God for making us special. To applaud the wisdom and magnanimity of the Creator is a way of appreciating His ingenuity in helping us discover our assignment with destiny, which happens only when man is in total cooperation with the Creator at work. This thinking underpins one of the laws of destiny: *Only when the students are ready is the teacher willing to appear, and only when the orphan is serious with honest striving do favours find a way to him.* God always works with the humblest and the most faithful. To celebrate our destiny is the only way we can tell God, "Thank you, thank you, thank you."

Think . . .

"Celebrating your destiny does not call for drinking, smoking, and other such merriment; instead it calls for deep reflection, deep appreciation, and great honour and service to the Creator, and it calls for a lot of prayers and thanksgiving to the founder and fountain of destiny."
Anthony U. Aliche

"It is not the critic who counts; not the man who points out how the strong man stumbles, or where the doer of deeds could have done them better. The credit belongs to the man who is actually in the arena, whose face is marred by dust and sweat and blood, who strives valiantly; who errs and comes short again and again; because there is not effort without error and shortcomings; but who does actually strive to do the deed; who knows the great enthusiasm, the great devotion, who spends himself in a worthy cause, who at the best knows in the end the triumph of high achievement and who at the worst, if he fails, at least he fails while daring greatly. So that his place shall never be with those cold and timid souls who know neither victory nor defeat."
Theodore Roosevelt

"Celebrating one's destiny is a way of thanking God."
Anthony U. Aliche

Chapter 26

Why is the destiny of Christmas known worldwide as the subject of the Infinite Trinity?

Many people are unfamiliar with the mystery of the jubilee of the Infinite Trinity. Even Christianity has not been able to appreciate the destiny of the Infinite, which is why religion has not been able to understand the glory, power, and mystery of Christmas as the sacramental ordinance that brings man to Christ, Christ to God, and God to humanity. It is at Christmas that the language and power of Infinite Trinity is celebrated as the glory of eternal destinies.

The destiny of Infinite Trinity can be defined as the glory eternally configured by God the Father, God the Son, and God the Holy Spirit, which became mystified with the command, "Let us create man in our own image."

A lot of people do not recognize Christmas as a destined event which brought to earth the glory of the celestial realms and brought to man the joy of the Lord. This joy, a supreme birth of destiny, has remained the foundation of Christianity.

If this foundation, which is a golden destiny, had not been led by God Himself and later celebrated by the angels, the beauty and the miracles of the Infinite Trinity could not have become part of Christmas.

When we celebrate Christmas, we are celebrating the achievement of the Infinite Trinity; the birth of the Golden Son of God; and the jubilee of the angels and the holy ones. Our celebration reminds us to appreciate the original meaning of Christmas, the meaning of destiny, and the sacrament of Infinite Trinity. It gives us hope to see Christ as our messiah, as light, as our destiny, as our glory, as our solace when all other hope is gone.

To those who understand the meaning and miracle of the Infinite Trinity, Christmas is the most significant event. It inspires us to seek, know, appreciate, and always reconcile ourselves with the jubilee of Christmas as the sacramental ordination of the Infinite Trinity.

When the Creator established the rein of the Infinite Trinity with the golden jubilee of Christmas, the blessed angels did not question or query Him, the holy ones and the saints only rejoiced, and Christ himself—the Consummate Destined Child of the Infinite Trinity—was gloriously lifted up to the mountaintop in accordance with the destiny of the origin of his lifting, which reads thus:

> *Behold thou universe of mine; behold thou destiny of all destinies; behold thou Christmas, which brought the consummation of the Infinite Trinity in action and reaction: this is my Destined Beloved Son, in whom I am well pleased, for he is eternally pleased in me as a way to show that he is the father in the son, the son in the father, the father in the spirit, and the spirit in the father and the son.*

This is why the lyrics of the famous Christian hymn reads thus:

> *Holy! Holy! Holy Lord God Almighty*
> *Early in the morning our song shall rise to thee.*
> *Holy! Holy! Holy.*
> *Merciful and mighty, God in three person*
> *Blessed Trinity.*

Christmas represents the joy of our life, the beauty of our soul, the power of our grace, and the wisdom of our knowledge and philosophy. We must remember that destiny, when properly discovered and utilized, presents a comprehensive balance sheet of our activities to the Creator. When there is no deficit in this balance sheet, the Creator says, "This is my beloved son in whom I am well pleased." This celestial and blessed statement has been used only once, in reference to Jesus Christ by God Himself, the powerful centre of the Infinite Trinity.

The inspired analogies in this chapter serve to buttress, showcase, explain, and praise the Infinite Trinity as the hallmark of Christmas. It is a means of enlightenment which reveals to our soul that when we discover our assignment with destiny, we are on the path of Christmas, on the Iliad-like path of divine mission. And we are under a strict mandate to use destiny, with its universal virtues, for service to the one-world family. The testimony of Jesus Christ is a case study of this selflessness and service.

The Infinite Trinity is like an iroko tree. It is a timeless billboard pointing to the way forward, directing us along the right path. This is why saints saw greatness in the star of Bethlehem, which led the wise men to visit the Holy Son, the fountain of Infinite Trinity. And it is why the angels rejoiced for the destiny of Christmas, which brought joy, faith, and good will to all men on earth, especially those who appreciate that Jesus is Lord.

A celebration of destiny with the Infinite Trinity is epitomized in a song that begins with the sacramental words, "immortal, invisible God only wise." **The meaning of this song** reinforces the theme of this chapter.

Humanity is blessed to have the opportunity to appreciate the destiny of the Infinite Trinity, the mystical foundry that brought the Jews and Gentiles to the throne of grace, the palace of glory, and the presence of God. Infinite Trinity defined the destiny of Christmas as the most important event since the dawn of consciousness.

23 December, 2010

Merry Xmas
&
A Prosperous New Year

Beloved Partners in Progress,

We are here to do this wonderful work because you are there to complement our great efforts.

As an author who is purpose-driven, enabled by the Creator's ingenious creativity, I have an obligation to convey a message of love from Christ, a message of truth from the angels, a message of wisdom from the saints, and, most important, a message of Christmas, a story that begins with the words *"Let there be light, and there was light."*

Many a man has not come to the full understanding that Christmas was the celestial current that destroyed the kingdom of darkness, thereby making us heirs to the kingdom of heaven.

Thanks be to God for the acceptance of our blessed Jesus Christ, who willingly, obediently, kindly, humbly, and loyally responded to his father's question, "Whom shall I send?" In doing so, he accomplished the wish and desire of his father, proclaiming, "Father, send me."

Many of us have not told our father, "Here I am, send me," but desplte that, we are celebrating the birth of a holy servant whose life and works stand as the pinnacle and beauty of the heavens. What a mystical Christ!

I feel highly blessed that I am able to give this Christmas message to all lovers of God. May the beauty and blessings of Christmas resound daily in our lives so that we always appreciate who God is and what Christ did for us. There is no better way to thank God for giving us His great servant, Christ the Saviour, than by worshiping His greatness in the beauty, purity, and perfection of Christmas, which has remained the greatest event since the dawn of consciousness.

If this message inspires you, kindly send it to others. If it does not, kindly reply back with an inspired Christmas message.

With these kind words which are drawn from my ingenious destined bank, may your Christmas gloriously spur you to a wonderful new year, a wonderful new life, and wonderful blessings from above. Let my words rekindle in you the sentiment inspired by one of the best-loved Christmas carols: Oh come let us adore Him!

Oh! Come all ye faithful,
Joyfully triumphant
To Bethlehem hasten now with glad accord
Lo in a manger, born the king of angels
Oh come let us adore him.
Oh come let us adore him
Oh come let us adore him, Christ the Lord.

Raise choirs of angels
Songs of loudest triumph
Through heaven's high archers be your praises poured
Now to our God be glory in the highest
Oh come let us adore him
Oh come let us adore him
Oh come let us adore him, Christ the Lord.

Amen! Lord we bless thee,
Born for our salvation
O Jesus! Forever be thy name adore
Word of the father, now in flesh appearing
Oh come let us adore him,
Oh come let us adore him
Oh come let us adore him, Christ the Lord. (SSS 31)

May you remain blessed in the jubilee and joy of Christmas.

Yours in light and with love,

Prof. Anthony Ugochukwu Aliche

(One of Professor Aliche's Christmas messages to the world)

Think . . .

"Religion has not been able to appreciate the destiny of the Infinite, which is why religion has not been able to understand the glory, power, and mystery of Christmas as the sacramental ordinance that brings man to Christ, Christ to God, and God to humanity. It is at Christmas that the language and power of Infinite Trinity is celebrated as the glory of eternal destinies.

"Behold thou universe of mine; behold thou destiny of all destinies; behold thou Christmas, which brought the consummation of the Infinite Trinity in action and reaction: this is my Destined Beloved Son, in whom I am well pleased, for he is eternally pleased in me as a way to show that he is the father in the son, the son in the father, the father in the spirit, and the spirit in the father and the son."
Anthony U. Aliche

Chapter 27

How does destiny reveal the story of birth and rebirth in a simple and humble way?

Destiny is both spiritually authoritative and humble in revealing the story of birth and the power of rebirth. That humility is infectious, making one immune to the lure of money and wealth.

A look at the way great geniuses and heroes are born reveals that this process is nothing but an anchor point in a glorious transition.

Few people have a thorough understanding of what birth is, and this chapter will explain with spiritual revelation the tenets that make birth a life mystery.

According to the psalms, the Creator is the symbol of our existence on earth; this is why He is spiritually significant to our own conception. The annunciation of the birth of Jesus Christ by the blessed angel Gabriel helps us understand the works of destiny and the revealing power of birth. No human being can be conceived, and no soul can be reincarnated into a spiritual form, if the greatest porter of ages, the supreme intelligence, is not at work to design and beautify the spiritual form before the womb can conceive and deliver.

The process of birth is always done at the behest of the Creator, who created man in His own image and gave Christ to us while we were yet sinners.

Of all the sciences man has established, only spiritual and astral biology offer a metaphysical explanation of how a woman conceives and how, by the authority of Mother Nature, she delivers when the time is right. A work examining the power of birth and rebirth in favour of destiny must be purpose-driven, with a focus on the Creator. This is so because all creations belong to Him, come from Him, and return to Him in due time, under the auspices of progressive destiny.

Through the concept of rebirth, destiny reminds us that we come and go. The processes of evolution, civilization, and growth reveal that man is intended to transcend. In one of my greatest works, *Birth and Rebirth: A Case Study of Man*, I explain that we are all tenants on earth, while the Creator is the consummate landlord; our life is a lease which can be revoked at any time when the owner wants it. The concept of birth and rebirth is ingenious; it is scientifically driven with the astral synergy of destiny. This is why destiny warns us always to be pure and clean, and to remember that our earthly life is temporary.

It is regrettable that so few people are conscious of their actions and reactions. That is why this book clearly states that any human being whose conscience is dead cannot fulfill the mission of destiny.

Have You Discovered Your Assignment with Destiny? is intended to make the reader understand that the philosophy and wisdom unraveled with birth and rebirth can be understood only when we know that destiny adheres strictly to the laws of birth and rebirth.

It is unfortunate that so many people do not understand the meaning of birth and rebirth, and that many are still in doubt about the concepts of incarnation and reincarnation. They must understand that we came from an original source, the Creator, and we must return to Him, the Universal One, in order to live a resourceful life.

Destiny uses our achievements to praise the Creator. The people we celebrate as geniuses, mystics, or gurus are those who used the discovery of their destiny to serve the world for the honour and glory of the Creator, fully realizing that birth and rebirth, life transition, and death are naturally propelled by destiny. This is why those who strive to discover their assignment with destiny are particularly humble; birth and rebirth are humble processes, and when these people leave the earth, their achievements, which are impeccable and unequalled, become perpetual solace and comfort for those left behind.

It is sheer stupidity not to understand the meaning of birth and rebirth; generation and regeneration; transition and re-transition. When we are in tune with the Infinite Mind, who propels our desires in accordance with our destiny, we discover that our lives work in harmony with the ministry of Jesus Christ; with the wonders of truth eternal; with the wisdom of our pilgrim fathers; with the knowledge of the apostles; and with the wisdom and philosophy of—*man how do you stand before your Creator?*

One of the immortal laws of birth and rebirth, which is in conjugal agreement with destiny, is that we must appreciate great gestures. If we don't, our ability to love will stagnate and our spiritual standing with the Creator will also stagnate and be undermined. This is why the science and concept of birth and rebirth, which are in synchronous agreement with destiny, remind us that every work of the Creator must be adored, respected, and honoured—because we live for God, we die for Christ, we transition to the angels, and we return to earthly life by the hands of the saints. Destiny always asks us these questions:

> *How well do you understand the meaning of birth and*
> *rebirth? Have you striven for greatness of destiny, so*
> *that people will proclaim that you are in tune with the*
> *wisdom of all ages, which reminds us that no condition is*
> *permanent?*

Think . . .

"Of all the sciences man has established, only spiritual and astral biology offer a metaphysical explanation of how a woman conceives and how, by the authority of Mother Nature, she delivers when the time is right."
Anthony U. Aliche

Chapter 28

How and why is your destiny formed by the spiritual power of God?

No human has the power, the knowledge, the wisdom, the fortune, the courage, and the spiritual intellect to manifest his destiny without the glorious and ingenious power of God's guidance. It has always been said that one with God is majority and that if you call God your father, He will in turn call you son.

The manifestation of our destiny cannot be possible without the power of God. That power directs our actions when we cooperate with the laws of God, the wisdom of Christ, and the laws of nature.

We cannot attract divine guidance as we journey in truth if our anchor does not rest with God.

A lot of people have abused, misplaced, rejected, and neglected their destiny because they use human power and academic intelligence in their spiritual quest for destiny; they don't realize that human wisdom is nothing but foolishness.

The power and strength of man do nothing but enslave him. That is why Jesus was very vocal in his command that Peter drop his sword. Our destiny cannot be made manifest if we are not constantly in touch with the electrifying currents of the heavens; if we are not obedient to God's laws; if we are not in total cooperation with the son of God, who is the equally glorious Son of man; if we do not appreciate the power of truth; if we are not in love with the wonderful works of the blessed angels, the saints, the holy ones, the Gideons, and the Gnostics. The heavens will never allow us to discover our destiny if our life is not driven by charitable instincts, shown in our service to God and humanity.

Solomon was never considered wise until he knew God and registered as a lifelong student of wisdom. When he was affected with wisdom, the power of God made him declare that all worldly things are vanity upon vanity.

Consider how God tackled Job with endless mystical and spiritual questions. In doing so, God revealed that his power is everything; that no man can detect nor direct him; and that destiny can be discovered only when, like Jesus Christ, we subject ourselves to the glorious feet of God.

Or consider how God made Abraham develop a destined faith, which in turn made Isaac be in tune with God. Destiny mandated that David would know that he could always do greater things with the power of God. The immortal power of destiny, which can be created and bestowed only by the Creator himself, made Jabez become a governor—evidence that with God we can rise from problems to praise; from grass to grace; from poverty to plenty.

The time has come for man to make the scriptures his goal, his constitution, and his anchor, because God decreed that all power in heaven and on earth belongs to His begotten son. In this context, Jesus Christ is designated as the rising sun, the eternal power of the East, and the immortal power of the North Star. This is why Jimmy Reeves sang so beautifully about the presence of God in every creation, in every man, in every age and era, when man simply cooperates with his Creator, the author of his destiny.

Kenneth Hagins notes that the power of God is at work as we reach old age, simply because we are finally cooperating with our destiny.

———

The philosophy of Dr. Walter Russell is practical and symbolically explained by Glenn Clark in his book, *The Man Who Talked with the Flowers*. Russell believed that when God is at work, destiny is at work, and when Christ is in charge, destiny is in command.

The power of God has remained an anchor point for those wishing to reach the treasure chest of destiny. When Moses and Joshua discovered their destiny, they accepted humbly, knowing full well that when God is at work, all works must be done with faith, truth, orderliness, and the joy of the Lord.

Paul's immortal contributions to Christianity after he had been a persecutor of the faithful shows that God can use his power to perform miracles, wonders, and signs. We know that when God is at work, the heavens must be opened; we discover that destiny is at work.

The time has come for people to appreciate the universal power of God; to understand the laws of destiny and their spiritual relationship to Christ and the celestial realms; to learn the mystical laws that formed the apostolic foundation of the Infinite Trinity. This is why from age to age, God's laws have revealed to us that He is mightier than any weapon or power. To behold him is to behold everything.

We can discover our destiny only when we understand that we have no power of our own and that we cannot walk alone, when we believe in the faith of Christ, the love of God, and the wisdom of our guardian and spiritual angels. This is what Christ meant when he stated that he and his father were one.

Think . . .

"The manifestation of our destiny cannot be possible without the power of God. That power directs our actions when we cooperate with the laws of God, the wisdom of Christ, and the laws of nature."

"Great thinkers know that destiny is a spiritual current from God and that its positive use creates enduring arts of which man is a real symbol of divine destiny."
Anthony U. Aliche

Chapter 29

What informed the celestial teachings surrounding mankind's beginning, the spiritual manifestation of your destiny?

It is time that people understand that their destiny is their heritage. It cannot be adulterated; it cannot be stolen; it cannot be stopped; it cannot be infiltrated. This is why noble souls work, love, and create with a sense of the origins of destiny.

Most people do not understand the infinite supremacy and spiritualism of destiny, that anything original is natural and spiritual. Since the dawn of consciousness, great minds have used destiny to become co-creators with the Infinite destined Intelligence, whose actions and transactions are original. This is why destiny can be utilized in answering the loftier question, What is beyond truth?

It is sad but true that many people envy, hate, gossip about, and even wish to kill those who have discovered their assignment with destiny. A lot of people do not recognize and act on the fact that the giver of destiny is the Supreme Master of the universe. The origin of destiny is naturally manifesting God and understanding the many purposes for which humans are destined.

It is important to explain that whoever does not use his destiny consciously to uplift the standard and welfare of humanity is enslaved; he has mortgaged his conscience. Such a person will certainly live to

---

regret his life on earth, because God anoints those He bestows with rare destinies.

The spiritual manifestation of destiny is revealed in our very beginning. Right from our mothers' womb, we are destined for something greater than mere words and actions. Those people we consider immortals were originally designated as co-creators with God, using the universal attributes of good character, love, and wisdom to ensure that their lives were purposefully and divinely inspired, used for the benefit of others and for the Creator.

The application of destiny in its spiritual originality reveals that we cannot do without destiny and we cannot do without God. The hands of destiny are naturally designated as the golden tree of life and the philosophical tree of knowledge.

From the time we start using our destiny, we join into a broader covenant with the Creator. The purpose of this covenant is to ignite the heavens to be our portion and providence.

A look at how destiny used Nelson Mandela for the people of South Africa, Kwame Nkrumah for the people of Ghana, and Albert Bongo for the people of Gabon, to name but a few examples, reinforces this celestial statement. By God's infallible and impeccable mercy, our destinies are designed for the use and application of achieving great things for the uplifting of humanity.

In our contemporary civilization, which is driven by political, social, economic, and human dynamics, destiny has called and uplifted Barack Obama to rise from the humblest of beginnings to the presidency of the topmost democracy in the world, the United States of America. In the same way, destiny has uplifted a classroom teacher named Dr. Goodluck Ebele Azikiwe Jonathan from the position of deputy governor of the smallest state in Nigeria to the vice presidency and, finally, the presidency of the most populous nation in Africa.

In the area of literature, destiny uplifted Wole Soyinka, who made a third class degree in the university, to become a Nobel laureate, and it designated William Shakespeare as the icon and giant of literary prowess.

Within the provinces of philosophy, religion, and theology there are Francis Bacon, Saints Thomas Aquinas, Augustine, Peter, and Paul, and our legendary contemporary Pope John II, one the most loved and gifted holders of the papacy. People will celebrate his golden life even into posterity; Christianity will never forget his destined achievements.

Destiny uplifted Bill Clinton to reorder the policies and ideals of the United States, greatly impacting the rest of the world, particularly the African continent. Even as the world was celebrating the turn of the millennium, we did not realize that Bill Gates was discovering new mysteries of destiny through his company Microsoft, which is working seriously to become a template for material globalization.

In Africa today, other great destined humans, like the author of this book, are now designated as famous, versatile, and ingenious. This author's creative and spiritual endeavours are extremely diverse, reinforcing the fact that our original beginning is the spiritual manifestation of destiny.

A lot of people do not understand the mystery of destiny—its meaning, purpose, definition, creative wisdom, and philosophy. Destiny follows a practical law: *Every man must show he that has been able to discover his assignment with destiny.*

This chapter would not be complete without a mention of the noble role of women in the universe. Their designation as the bearers of beauty, the backbone of the family, the maker of great heroes and kings, serves to explain their role and calling in creation. Role models like Mary Slessor, Florence Nightingale, Philippines Aquinas, Ellen Sirleaf, Queen Elizabeth of England, Indira Gandhi, and Lao Russell, along with other queens of the planetary heritage, must be remembered as part of the original beginning, spiritually manifested through the ingenuity of destiny.

The light of destiny is more powerful than the wisdom of the saints. The strength and wisdom of destiny form a celestial current which cannot be explained by man. Buttressing this statement are the lives of the Twelve World Teachers, the immortal geniuses, the Gideons, and others spiritually grounded in that original beginning of the supreme manifestation of destiny. Their lives are the actualization of the celestial mandate, a wake-up call reminding us that a life lived without discovering our assignment with destiny is a wasted life.

Think . . .

"Whoever does not use his destiny consciously to uplift the standard and welfare of humanity is enslaved; he has mortgaged his conscience. Such a person will certainly live to regret his life on earth, because God anoints those he bestows with rare destinies."
Anthony U. Aliche

"We are not permitted to choose the frame of our destiny. But what we put into it is ours."
Dag Hammarskjold

"Destiny is something not to be desired and not to be avoided, a mystery not contrary to reason, for it implies that the world, and the course of human history, have meaning."
Dag Hammarskjold

"Give up the feeling of responsibility, let go your hold, resign the care of your destiny to higher powers, be genuinely indifferent as to what becomes of it all, and you will find not only that you gain a perfect inward relief, but often also, in addition, the particular goods you sincerely thought you were renouncing."
William James

Chapter 30

How does the discovery of our destiny bring us gloriously to the wisdom of all ages?

The immortal words of Socrates, "Let him that would move the world first move himself," are echoed in the nineteenth-century rhyme, "If everyone will see to his own reformation, how very easily you might reform a nation."

Many people do not understand the meaning, purpose, wisdom, and philosophy contained in our ability to discover our destiny, and especially how this rare knowledge can bring us to the wisdom of all ages.

It is important at this point to ask ourselves, What is the wisdom of all ages, and what are its philosophy, purpose, content, concept, rhythm, and contributions to evolution since the dawn of consciousness?

Simply put, the wisdom of all ages is the consummate light that gave life meaning, function, and authority. In some higher quarters and great schools of thought, the wisdom of all ages is defined symbolically—as the power of truth, for example, or the wish of light, or the glory and greatness of the Creator. It is the knowledge of all things, the power of evolution, and the consummate spirituality of the known and unknown.

Destiny respects wisdom and its ability to transform a system, a nation, a family, or an institution because nothing is greater. Everything exists within and revolves around wisdom. Destiny, being part of the creative wisdom of all ages, must be used in accordance with the rhythm, power, and principle of all ages.

You must understand the real meaning of destiny as it relates to the authoritative ingenuity of wisdom—particularly balanced wisdom that is dynamic and creative.

The authority and power of destiny reveal that all ages are destined to appreciate wisdom, which in turn appreciates the wisdom of all ages.

This chapter focuses on the proper understanding of the labeling of history, the path of history, and the achievements and impact of history. We have a mandate to remember history's great thinkers, whose contributions have shaped human civilization. Our evolution and growth, all our achievements and conquests reveal how they used destiny to overcome challenges and achieve success.

Wisdom and destiny are intertwined and positively related. This is why many people consider destiny an abstract notion, just as they might see wisdom as a mighty ocean whose depths and size are beyond ordinary comprehension. The wisdom of all ages is best understood when we discover our assignment with destiny and appreciate destiny's power; when we use the rhythm of destiny to provide honest service; and when we think positively and universally to ensure that we transform people's lives through the application of our destined wisdom.

Perhaps the most difficult mission in all areas of human endeavor is the task of reforming people, educating them, and understanding human psychology. This challenge is what inspired Edwin Markham to say that "against making cities we should make man."

Ralph Waldo Emerson and Dr. Walter Russell voiced a similar concern when they stated, "In vain we build the cities without building man."

The content of this and the previous two chapters reinforces the fact that it is difficult to behold, control, utilize, and understand destiny at a practical level. In its thematic wisdom lie the secrets of light, life, and dynamic achievements, including the living secrets of all ages. These secrets cannot be taught in the universities, because the lessons therein involve knowledge far more powerful than any academic curriculum.

In fact, most of those great people who used their destiny to understand the wisdom of all ages were not good students. Most were not doctors or professors, and some were not even considered intellectuals. Instead, they were inspired by the secret wisdom of all ages, which they then adopted as a business necessity. That wisdom caused them to face life in a pragmatic way, practicing truth and honouring wisdom.

The legacy left by Solomon, with his definition and discovery of wisdom, cannot be fully understood or explained without considering the wonders and mystery of destiny. He discovered his destiny through the revelation of the Almighty, having tested life, particularly its material aspects, and decided that all egocentric and worldly things make no meaning.

When we use our destiny to appreciate and discover the monumental wisdom of all ages, our life is spiritually transformed. Our ideas and concepts about life become universal and positive, and we silently detach from the activities of the crowd, the voices of the uninformed, and the practices of pagans. The inspired genius that destiny reawakens within us makes us question most of the activities of the church, and we begin applying some of the principles of destiny in order to see things as they are. Destiny becomes the authority, as it should be.

The wisdom of all ages lives in the glorious powers of destiny, which is the original genius that makes us appreciate the wisdom of God, the secrets of light, and the sacred teachings of all ages. This pattern of life motivates us to respect wisdom and honour the powers and philosophy of divine nature.

When properly discovered and utilized, destiny has always led humans along the noble path toward honest knowledge, a balanced life, and truthful practices, freeing us from bondage and enslavement.

The purpose of this chapter is to point out that only destiny, with its objective and balanced way of teaching us, is capable of helping us appreciate, understand, and use the wisdom of all ages, which is the wisdom of truth, knowledge, power, light, and love. With the discovery of our destiny, we can gloriously and generously thank God for making us special, because that discovery is a sacred and unique task. The understanding and utilization of the wisdom of all ages is also a sacred and unique assignment; its fruitful achievement lies in understanding that genius is an inherent wisdom that can be known and practiced only when we personally and humbly submit to the wish, will, and consummate wisdom of the Creator.

Think . . .

"The immortal words of Socrates, 'Let him that would move the world first move himself,' are echoed in the nineteenth-century rhyme, 'If everyone will see to his own reformation, how very easily you might reform a nation.'"
Anthony U. Aliche

"Our destiny exercises its influence over us even when, as yet, we have not learned its nature: it is our future that lays down the law of our today."
Friedrich Nietzsche

Chapter 31

Is it true that the power, wisdom, and knowledge of destiny are more useful and fruitful than the wisdom of academics?

Destiny, as we know, is made gloriously fruitful with the use and application of balanced wisdom, divine love, creative achievements, and inspired understanding. This is why all academic knowledge combined cannot and will not approach the consummate wonders and greatness of destiny.

Socrates, an enlightened teacher of the highest genius, is designated as an electrifying current of knowledge whose imaginative powers were beyond academic reason. Similar thinkers from different and glorious planes of life have made a sojourn on this planet and used the wisdom of destiny to establish immortal empires of knowledge as well as schools of provincial thought. Since the dawn of consciousness, destiny has remained the only way by which humans can have a fulfilled life.

It is important to reflect on the life and times of the Twelve World Teachers, the immeasurable contributions of the great philosophers and mystics who were able to discover their academic missions with destiny. In his highly rated work *America's Assignment with Destiny*, Manly Hall praises Isaiah's prophetic statement that was manifested when Christopher Columbus was inspired to establish the kingdom of a New World beyond the ecstasy of time and the wisdom of space. Intellectualism, despite its academic excellence, is hobbled by limitations, by the use of empirical concepts and ideas, and by a lack of objective reasoning. Destiny is both surgery and surgeon, an impeccable dominion whose wisdom is beyond words and thoughts, and whose creations are characterized by the best use of purity and perfection. This is why creation is hereby defined as a crystal consummation of perfect destiny.

The joy and jubilee of Christmas, whose mysteries, mysticism, and cosmic metaphysics defy academia, reveal that humans celebrate the creativity of destiny, but in a ceremonial way. It is a deluge of emotions born out of man's wonderful ambition to appreciate and understand the meticulous definition of destiny, reflected in the story of Christmas. A book conveying the urgent necessity of discovering our academic mission with destiny, and distinguishing it from mere academic excellence, must appreciate the fact that destiny is a consummate virtue and gift. From time to time, the Oriental wizards would look upon their ingenious creations and appreciate destiny as a glorious star, a wonderful sacrament. With that in mind, humans should ask themselves these questions:

- What is destiny?
- What is the meaning of destiny?
- Can I define destiny?
- What is my destiny?
- How can I define my destiny?
- How can I discover my destiny as a talent, a gift, or a grace, and how can I ensure that the impact of destiny becomes my legacy?
- Can I steal destiny? If so, how can I use it?
- Why is the work of destiny a great mystery?
- Why do we celebrate the achievements of destiny?
- Why is an honest life gloriously fulfilled through the use and application of destiny?
- Why is destiny considered a great teacher?
- Why is the Creator the beacon of ingenious destiny?
- How and why does destiny consider academic excellence robotic?

- Who in contemporary society serves as an example of someone who has discovered his academic gift through destiny?
- Is destiny the gift given to one person or a universal gift to all humanity?
- What are the ladder, the wisdom, and the achievements of destiny? Why does this book compare destiny to a beautiful country established on abundant land whose fields are naturally endowed with nature's glories?

Reflecting on these questions makes a great impact on us, leaving no doubt in the mind of the enlightened that destiny is beyond the scope of ordinary knowledge. It surpasses academic excellence; intellectual prowess cannot compete with or even come near its electrifying powers. Such great thinkers as Michael Faraday, a pioneer in the study of electricity; Albert Einstein, the genius of scientific ingenuity; Mozart, the composer of ingenious songs and solos; Plato, famous for his powerful philosophical creativity; and Jesus Christ, who used destiny and spiritual ingenuity to crush the demons of human enmity, are hereby designated as supreme ecclesiastical icons among destined beings. Their missionary impact still rules the world, still governs the seen and unseen. This is why this chapter aims to explain that destiny is a conqueror whose victory cannot be mathematically quantified with figures, data, and statistics, but instead is gloriously established in facts. We are all invited to the garden of nature's destiny, but we can access it only when natural law and spiritual desire drive our thoughts, our philosophy, and our principles. We must not believe that academic law rules all creation.

Think . . .

"Destiny is beyond the scope of ordinary knowledge. It surpasses academic excellence; intellectual prowess cannot compete with or even come near its electrifying powers."
Anthony U. Aliche

"It can't help but have some effect. But at the end of the day you have to be master of your own destiny, not looking at what everyone else is doing . . . if the others drop the ball, well and good, but ultimately you can't rely on that. You've got to design a car that's quicker than theirs."
Mike Gascoyne

"Intellectualism, despite its academic excellence, is hobbled by limitations, by the use of empirical concepts and ideas and a lack of objective reasoning. Destiny is both surgery and surgeon, an impeccable dominion whose wisdom is beyond words and thoughts, and whose creations are characterized by the best use of purity and perfection."
Anthony U. Aliche

Chapter 32

Why is destiny known by the Orientals as the apostolic expression and manifestation of God's ingenuity?

This question is best answered with other, more objective questions, in keeping with the title and theme of this book: Have you discovered your assignment with destiny? There are several questions that can serve as a guide in buttressing and explaining the concepts in chapter 31, producing a coherent narrative of the beautiful role of destiny in our lives.

To that end, ask yourself the following questions:

- Who is God?
- What is God?
- What is beyond God?
- What is the authority of God?
- Why Is God everything and in all things?
- Why is God the beginning of immortality and the dominant wisdom of consummate immortality?
- Why is God's hand the symbol of destiny?
- Why is creative destiny God's sign?
- Why is destiny the sign of God's universal excellence?
- Why is this destiny a determining factor in creating excellent and immortal concepts that will stand the test of time and withstand human wisdom and educational philosophy?

———————

- Why is destiny bigger than today or tomorrow, an ingenious technology of posterity?

The Orientals know destiny as the apostolic philosophy of the expression and manifestation of God's ingenuity, because destiny comes from God—it is God practically manifested. Destiny can also be defined as the manifestation of God when man cooperates with Him. Every age has had highly enlightened beings who work to actualize their desire through the use and application of their destiny. This is why the apostolic foundation of all the strongest institutions is aligned with God's glorious destiny, which is seed of faith and a shower of blessings.

When we discover our destiny, our human weaknesses become a thing of the past. Our mortality, our lack of faith in God, our lack of wisdom—all are abolished simply because the application of destiny makes us live in the objective and creative light of the all-knowing. Destiny is above human senses, human creativity, human knowledge, and material things and philosophies. Throughout all eras, only God has showered blessings upon all who desire to know their divine mandate and make an honest bid for those blessings by knocking and asking for them. Those gifts must be used to serve, to uplift the downtrodden and the less privileged. At its highest level, destiny is spiritual, not material.

Those within the academic community may be surprised to learn that the best intellectuals have not discovered their assignment with destiny. Academia is polluted by lapses in information, lapses that have engulfed people's natural intellectual mechanism, making them believe that material education is the pinnacle of success.

To destiny, this is a taboo, an inglorious story that has created a tremendous lack of understanding and wisdom. Intellectuals now battle with uncreative concepts, lopsided ideas, meaningless notions which are as old as time itself. This should serve as an admonition to those who would want to pattern their lives on those of the great thinkers within the annals of destiny.

The apostolic creativity and fraternity of destiny, when well understood and utilized, brings us to the corridor of all knowledge, to ultimate certainty and success, and to the immortality of our creative dynamism. The way the first Christian apostles were ordained by and worked with destiny when they were initiated at Pentecost reveals that the force of destiny is as mighty as the ocean.

It is the honest goal of this chapter to make all and sundry appreciate that God is the maker, the giver, and the owner of destiny. Since the dawn of consciousness, only a few humans have been able to discover their assignment, which is governed by the following eternal laws:

- the law of destiny
- the law of truth
- the law of obedience
- the law of sacrifice
- the laws of charity
- the law of giving and receiving
- the law of balance
- the law of exchange and interchange
- the law of honesty and courage to be a brother's keeper
- the law of homogeneity
- the law of attraction of species
- the law of give and take
- the law of knowing and knowledge
- the law of wisdom and wizardry.

The most important laws of destiny are all galvanized by the electrifying laws of divinity, honesty, achievements, fruitful thoughts, objective creativity, understanding, peace, and harmony. Destiny is always against those who are naturally wicked, weak, dishonest, or egocentric, or those whose ideas and concepts are far from the wisdom of God.

Have you discovered your assignment with destiny? Your answer to that question is tied to several others: Who is your God and how do you emulate Him? How do you communicate with Him? How does He direct you? Have you been baptised by the flame of inspiration?

The apostolic creativity of destiny asks us these questions:

- Who are you?
- What are you?
- Why are you here?
- Who made the world?
- Who made man?
- Who made the seas, the mountains, the forests, the air, the deserts, the planets, the firmaments, and the seas?

This chapter is practically titled to remind us that the creativity of destiny is spiritually symbolic. *The day you discover your assignment with destiny marks the beginning of your harmonious relationship with your Creator, the beginning of your understanding of God and human nature.* It is when you begin thinking cosmically and acting universally. The Orientals, in their enlightenment, appreciated, revered, and worshipped God for the beauty of His ingenious and consummate destiny. This book is best understood within the realm of discovering your true self in order to know and appreciate why we are empowered to experience the wonders and beauties of earthly life. When practically and purposefully fulfilled, our destiny returns us to the eternal kingdom where God's grace flows through us. When properly harnessed, the lessons, wonders, impact, and understanding of destiny make the giver appreciate us with a celestial welcome into that eternal paradise of destiny, which is full of beauty, joy, mercy, and grace. We must accept the desire for destiny as a divine and earthly mandate.

This chapter reveals that a lot of people are far from really understanding destiny. In ancient times, the urge to find and fulfill one's destiny was considered the highest and greatest occupation. Even today, the challenge to know, appreciate, and use our destiny is the only way we can work knowingly with the Creator, who is everything in all things. He is the absolute beacon of destiny, which when known, discerned, and utilized makes one a genius of his time. So destiny invites us all to seek, to knock, and to ask, and to understand that he that seeketh more is he that will be given the best.

Have You Discovered Your Assignment with Destiny? brings together the wisdom of the apostolic manifestation of God's ingenuity both known and unknown, in the past and in the future. Hence destiny is galvanized as the creative ingenuity of all ages.

Think . . .

"The Orientals know destiny as the apostolic philosophy of the expression and manifestation of God's ingenuity, because destiny comes from God—it is God practically manifested. Destiny can also be defined as the manifestation of God when man cooperates with Him."

"God's ingenuity in you opens all doors for you.
Seek it, ask for it, and utilize it.
Then will you be truly happy."
Anthony U. Aliche

A General Overview of This Book

In writing this overview, it is important to praise, obey, and appreciate the only Creator of destiny, who in the aesthetic semblance of man glorified Himself as the beacon of His ingenuity with destiny. It is unfortunate that so few people have been able to identify with their own destiny. We are living in a world that does not strive to use or appreciate the free dominion of destiny, which is beyond words and thoughts and above all academic and intellectual realms.

This book starts by introducing an honest question; it then delves into a philosophical discussion whose wisdom and purpose will certainly ignite the mind of the reader and inspire him to go on a quest for his own destiny, beginning with another honest question, "God, must I go empty-handed?" This question reflects the emotional and thoughtful entreaty of sailors in the Spanish Armada, who intuitively discovered that they could be used despite their situation to give the world great gifts.

The beauty and practicality of the preceding pages, which also can be downloaded, have Ignited a call to appreciate the definition of destiny, to recognize its origin and power and the source of its wisdom, and to understand why man is a subject of destiny.

These inspired chapters challenge all readers to see that destiny is the way of the Creator, the power of life, and the wisdom of light and all life. These chapters form a great dominion of impeccable wisdom, beginning with three questions: Have you discovered your assignment with destiny? What have you used your destiny to achieve for creation? And who has benefited from your destiny?

Chapter 9, a guide for those who do not understand what destiny is all about, started by asking readers why they are allowing their destiny and time to be wasted. This chapter was inspired by the urge to understand the purpose and philosophy of Africa, the continent's assignments with destiny, and the practical lessons of these assignments. Chapters 12 to 20 offer a meticulous explanation, asking humanity to seek and to knock, to be courageous and determined in its search for destiny. A highlight of this section is chapter 17, whose title reads thus: Do the scriptures give a genealogical account of men who discovered their assignment with destiny, and how are those genealogies chronicled? The chapter is both a symbolic challenge and a spiritual mandate.

Chapter 21 begins by explaining why destiny is the mission of love fulfilled. By maintaining that destiny is the bread of love, the bread of life, and the sacrament of authority, it leads the way to chapters 22 to 29.

The last chapter can be defined as an eloquent amalgamation of destiny, a scientific epilogue with consummate wisdom and ingenious reasoning. It highlights the lives of a few humans as examples of those who actively sought out their assignment with destiny, reminding us that destiny is the ultimate consummation of our relationship with the Creator.

I must acknowledge the immortal contributions of Mike Omoleye. His book *You Can Control Your Destiny* was seen as a flame of authority for other writers like Manly Palmer Hall, who wrote *America's Assignment with Destiny*. The first book and first love of Dr. Walter Russell are reflected in his immortal work, which reminds us that genius is inherent in every man. Along with his wonderful wife Lao Russell, he wrote a book on destiny which explains that God can work with you but not for you. The book challenges us to ask for our own destiny and to make destiny a luminous partner in our progress.

No book can offer an adequately and comprehensive overview of what destiny is, because no man has authorship of God, just as no man has authorship of the air and sea. God's creations are the symbolic fruit of His destiny, the embodiment of His destiny, the seeding and semblance of what makes Him the Creator. This is why the honest challenge of writing this book, intended as a purposeful partner for humanity, is a great assignment destined to be fulfilled, honoured, and achieved. Because when humans discover their assignment with destiny, the world will be propelled by purpose-driven life.

This overview does not fully explore the wonders and greatness of destiny as a force and light from the fragmental current of the consummate Creator, but it helps explain the order of divinely inspired ecstasy. This is why your destiny is a teacher of truth, a comprehensive mandate to be fulfilled and accomplished. To answer the call of destiny is the only way we can return a practical and perfect thank you to the Creator for making us special, for creating us in His image, for blending and blessing us with the beauty of the angels.

A look at the greatness of destiny makes us appreciate it as the wisdom that created the composite wonders of the omnipotent, the omnipresent, omni-scientific ecstasy of one whose destiny is driven by purpose and balanced creativity. And man is the perfect pinnacle of that destined ingenuity.

Other Quotes from the Mighty and Enriched Bank of Destiny

"Nature has plenty of open banks for those who want to invest in it."
Anthony U. Aliche

"Desire and God are all you need to discover your destiny."
Anthony U. Aliche

"A true man never frets about his place in the world, but just slides into it by the gravitation of his nature, and swings there as easily as a star."
Edwin Hubbel

"Destiny is something we've invented because we can't stand the fact that everything that happens is accidental."
Albert SchweiTser

"Anything that happens once does not necessarily happen again. Everything that happens twice is likely to happen for the third time as well."
Arab Quote

"If you only do what you know you can do—you never do very much."
Tom Krause

"Don't wait. The time will never be just right."
Napoleon Hill

"Contemplation often makes life miserable. We should act more, think less, and stop watching ourselves live."
Nicolas Chamfort

"Our dead brothers still live for us and bid us think of life, not death—of life to which in their youth they lent the passion and glory of Spring. As I listen, the great chorus of life and joy begins again, and amid the awful orchestra of seen and unseen powers and destinies of good and evil, our trumpets, sound once more a note of daring, hope, and will."
Oliver Wendell Holmes

"The first point was we wanted power to determine our own destiny in our own black community. And what we had done is, we wanted to write a program that was straightforward to the people. We didn't want to give a long dissertation."
Bobby Seale

"What we may be seeing is a real cultural shift in the UK with more people looking for control over their own destiny and working their socks off for themselves rather than someone else, as opposed to striving for power and money by moving up the corporate ladder."
John Davis

"There is nothing left worth preserving in the notions of unseen powers, controlling human destiny, to which obedience and worship are due."
John Dewey

"The San are no longer masters of their destiny. They can no longer practice hunting and gathering, something the government could have tried to correct when it came into power sixteen years ago."
Ben Ulenga

"Remember, a Jedi's strength flows from the Force. But beware. Anger, fear, aggression. The dark side are they. Once you start down the dark path, forever will it dominate your destiny. Luke . . . Luke . . . do not . . . do not underestimate the powers of the Emperor or suffer your father's fate you will. Luke, when gone am I . . . the last of the Jedi will you be. Luke, the Force runs strong in your family. Pass on what you have learned, Luke. There is . . . another . . . Sky . . . walker."

"Some world powers are used to subjugating other nations to their own will, but they should realize that the era of domination has passed, and the time has come for the peoples of the world to direct their own destinies."
Mahmoud Ahmadinejad

"The problem we have is that we have no power—in regards to controlling our own destiny—we can't even get the county assessor to come up here."
Mike Hess

"Man's ultimate destiny is to become one with the Divine Power which governs and sustains the creation and its creatures."
Alfred A. Montapert

"The spirit and determination of the people to chart their own destiny is the greatest power for good in human affairs."
Matt Blunt

"The thirst for adventure is the vent which Destiny offers; a war, a crusade, a gold mine, a new country, speak to the imagination and offer swing and play to the confined powers."
Ralph Waldo Emerson

"Black Power is giving power to people who have not had power to determine their destiny."
Huey Newton

"Music conveys moods and images. Even in opera, where plots deal with the structure of destiny, it's music, not words, that provides power."
Marcel Marceau

"We have destiny in our hands. If we take care of our business, we don't need any help. That's what makes it, on the positive side, a good game. We don't need anybody else to do anything."
Tom Izzo

"We're in a position where we can control our own destiny. We don't need anybody to help us out. We've just got to win a series next weekend, finish up on the right note, and get us to the post season."
Brian Blessie

"Beating Arizona Lutheran puts us in the driver's seat in the conference. It helps us in terms of we can control our own destiny at this point. We just have to stay focused and continue to improve because those teams will be improving each week, too."
Bill Morgan

"It was just nice all around play tonight. The kids got a lead and then kept their composure. The Peru game really helped prepare us for Western's pressure. We now have control over our own destiny in the conference."
Rick Clark

"It can't help but have some effect. But at the end of the day you have to be master of your own destiny, not looking at what everyone else is doing . . . if the others drop the ball, well and good, but ultimately you can't rely on that. You've got to design a car that's quicker than theirs."
Mike Gascoyne

"If we play the way we can, we still can help control our own destiny."
Bobby Perry

"I believe that the people, instead of pretty lies, should be told the truth, no matter how ugly it may be. What can we do, destiny hasn't been kind to us; but, with the help of God, we will prevail."
Alija Izetbegovic

"Traveling is all very well if you can get home at night. I would be willing to go around the world if I came back in time to light the candles and set the table for supper. I cannot conceivably influence the world's destiny, but I can make my own life more worthwhile. I can give some help to some people; that is not vital to all the world's problems, and yet I think if everyone did just that, we might see quite a world in our time!"
Gladys Taber

"Poor people cannot rely on the government to come to help you in times of need. You have to get your education. Then nobody can control your destiny."
Charles Barkley

"I believe it is a genuine expression of the will of the international community, led by the Security Council, to come together again after last year's divisions and to help the Iraqi people take charge of their own political destiny—in peace and freedom—under a sovereign government."
Kofi Annan

••

"It's choice—not chance—that determines your destiny."
Jean Nidetch

"There is no such thing as an omen. Destiny does not send us heralds. She is too wise or too cruel for that."
Oscar Wilde

"It is a mistake to look too far ahead. Only one link in the chain of destiny can be handled at a time."
Winston Churchill

"The best years of your life are the ones in which you decide your problems are your own. You do not blame them on your mother, the ecology, or the president. You realize that you control your own destiny."
Albert Ellis

"Sometimes being a friend means mastering the art of timing. There is a time for silence. A time to let go and allow people to hurl themselves into their own destiny. And a time to prepare to pick up the pieces when it's all over."
Gloria Naylor

"It's not what's happening to you now or what has happened in your past that determines who you become. Rather, it's your decisions about what to focus on, what things mean to you, and what you're going to do about them that will determine your ultimate destiny."
Anthony Robbins

"The high destiny of the individual is to serve rather than to rule . . ."
Albert Einstein

"A man who has depths in his shame meets his destiny and his delicate decisions upon paths which few ever reach . . ."
Friedrich Nietzsche

"I can't control my destiny, I trust my soul, my only goal is just to be. There's only now, there's only here. Give in to love or live in fear. No other path, no other way. No day but today."
Jonathan Larson

"It's within the ability of the Liberian people to seize their destiny . . . Unless he's brought to the bar of justice, eventually all of West Africa will be in jeopardy. And Nigeria won't be immune."
Ed Royce

"Our destinies are absolutely intertwined. Africa is absolutely fundamental for the South African economy."
Alec Erwin

"The law of harvest is to reap more than you sow. Sow an act, and you reap a habit. Sow a habit and you reap a character. Sow a character and you reap a destiny."
James Allen

"The destinies of the two races in this country are indissolubly linked together, and the interests of both require that the common government of all shall not permit the seeds of race hate to be planted under the sanction of law."
Bobby Scott

"Love, the strongest and deepest element in all life, the harbinger of hope, of joy, of ecstasy; love, the definer of all laws, of all conventions; love, the freest, the most powerful moulder of human destiny; how can such an all-compelling force be synonymous with that poor little State and Church-begotten weed, marriage?"
Emma Goldman

"Destiny, in its ingenuity, tells the world that every noble woman is a product of the universal foundry. This is why only women are the supreme mothers of the universe."
Anthony U. Aliche

"Destiny, in its immortal maxim, defined a woman as the mother of the universe, the mother of the greatest man in creation. This is why the rise and fall of every man is destined to happen with the involvement of a noble woman."
Anthony U. Aliche

"Out of love for the thought and power of destiny, my mother told me that the original cells of her life come from the character of her destiny."
Anthony U. Aliche

"Destiny defined a family circle as a living business of two equal partners. This is what informed and empowered Lao Russell to authoritatively write her great work entitled *The Electrifying Power of Man-Woman Balance*, which is known as the equality of all species."
Anthony U. Aliche

"Since the creation of man, only a half percent of humans have discovered and fulfilled their assignment with destiny."
Anthony U. Aliche

"Every human being who wants to achieve his assignment with destiny must be determined to make the waves of inspiration his business necessity."
Anthony U. Aliche

"Destiny provided the ladder with which Nelson Mandela rose from prison to presidency.
The star of destiny diligently empowered Goodluck Jonathan to rise from the lecture hall to the presidency."
Anthony U. Aliche

"A. U Aliche, with authoritative and ingenious dynamism toward the province of destiny, was driven to establish a vast bank naturally mandated as a museum of knowledge for the balanced wisdom of posterity and consummate destiny, which will live to the glory of human evolution and immortality."
Anthony U. Aliche

"Your enemies' action can ignite an action for you to locate your destiny."
Anthony U. Aliche

"Challenge is a catalyst that ignites the forceful action of destiny."
Anthony U. Aliche

"The day you discover your assignment with destiny is the day you discover your mission for life."
Anthony U. Aliche

"Mary Slessor, the destined arrowhead for the cessation of the killing of twins, said that her destiny is to stop their massacre because no one can know who will be the next Christ."
Anthony U. Aliche

"Destiny told the world that the training of one female is the training and empowerment of the whole universe."
Anthony U. Aliche

"Destiny can never be at work without the ingenuity of Mother Nature."
Anthony U. Aliche

"Tell me what your destiny is, and I will certainly tell you what your success is going to be."
Anthony U. Aliche

"Eternal success is the consummate product of destiny."

Anthony U. Aliche

"The songs and melodies of destiny are eternal, rhyming with the authoritative wisdom of consummate destiny."
Anthony U. Aliche

"Those who are anointed with the light and wisdom of destiny are defined as pure souls from the realm of perfect destiny."
Anthony U. Aliche

"Jesus talked about the power of destiny in the Sermon on the Mount, often referred to as the Beatitudes."
Anthony U. Aliche

"To the one God, the consummate Universal One, be the glory and honour for giving man the power and praises of Destiny, which is the only authority that makes him discover his inherent genius and then put it to effective use."
Anthony U. Aliche

"Call me a child of destiny; define me as an ingenious symbol of destiny. All my actions and creations will say amen, for Jesus is the ornamented child and the physician of the divine destiny for which my life is purpose-driven."
Anthony U. Aliche

"Have you asked yourself what your destiny is, and what you are destined for?"
Anthony U. Aliche

"Rev. King was destined to stop racism and discrimination, which were prevalent in the American system of old."
Anthony U. Aliche

"Bill Clinton told the world he was destined to make the white race appreciate the value of the black race. This is what inspired him to initiate the universal visa lottery."
Anthony U. Aliche

"Those who work against destiny only cultivate the root of permanent adversity in their own lives and destiny."
Anthony U. Aliche

"The thought of destiny is an inspirational force for the creation of permanent ideas."
Anthony U. Aliche

"It is the power of destiny that shapes and measures your success."
Anthony U. Aliche

"When God calls you blessed, destiny calls you a holy one."
Anthony U. Aliche

Appendixes

Poet's Code of Ethics

Inspired by Herbert Spencer and His Aborigines

- ❑ To attain the brotherhood of man idea by taking righteous action and showing good will toward every man instead of taking from him that which he has
- ❑ To discover that all men are extensions of each other, that man is made for man, and that the hurt of one man is the hurt of all men
- ❑ To develop character, intelligence, and good citizenship by teaching every man from early youth how to be a good neighbour and a loyal citizen
- ❑ To discover one's inner self by awakening within him that spark of divine genius which lies dormant in every man
- ❑ To teach man to think rather than to remember and repeat
- ❑ To realize that work done for the material world should be for man's ennoblement, not for grinding his soul out in the gears of industrial machines
- ❑ to know that man is mind, not body, that he is immortal spirit, not flesh, that he is good, not bad
- ❑ To judge the righteousness and religion of any man by what he does to his fellow man, and not by his beliefs, doctrines, creeds, or dogmas
- ❑ To give a scientific course of study for comprehension of the Spencer Code of Human Relations as the inviolate law of

---

God, which man knows he must obey or else pay the price in personal unhappiness and international wars

❑ To teach the scientific meaning of "Seek ye the Kingdom of Heaven within you"; "I and my Father are one"; "God is Light, God is Love"; "What I am, ye also are"; and "What I do, ye can also do."

Lao Russell's Code of Ethics for a Living Philosophy

- ❑ To bring blessing upon yourself, bless your neighbour.
- ❑ To enrich yourself, enrich your neighbour.
- ❑ Honour your neighbour and your neighbour will honour you.
- ❑ To sorely hurt yourself, hurt your neighbour.
- ❑ He who seeks love will find it by giving it.
- ❑ The measure of a man's wealth is the measure of wealth he has given.
- ❑ To enrich yourself with many friends, enrich your friends with your self.
- ❑ That which you take away from any man the world will take away from you.
- ❑ When you take the first step to give yourself to that which you want, it will also take the first step to give itself to you.
- ❑ Peace and happiness do not come to you from your horizon. They spread from you out to infinity beyond your horizon.
- ❑ The whole universe is a mirror which reflects back to you that which you reflect into it.
- ❑ Love is like unto the ascent of a high mountain peak, it comes ever nearer to you as you go ever nearer to it.

Professor Aliche's Living Code of Ethics for the Modern Generation

❑ Guard yourself against doing evil by either omission or commission.

❑ Stand on a good institution, which will represent you and your generations to come.

❑ Think good of your neighbour and the world will think good of you.

❑ Speak no evil, see no evil, and hear no evil.

❑ Maintain an ethic of love and peace to guide you to good public relations.

❑ Show love to everybody, and ensure that peace governs all your life with truth and love.

❑ Envy no one to avoid anyone envying you.

❑ See the good in others, and emulate the best you see in the world.

❑ Work to perfect your talents, and see the beauties in creation as goals waiting for you to attain them.

❑ Help the needy and the helpless, and see to it that your help is without harm to those that need it.

❑ Develop your faith with sound courage and positive judgment.

❑ Avoid committing karma so that you and your generations will not suffer from your karmic burden.

❑ Speak well of your neighbour, yourself, and the world, and maintain discipline at all times.

❑ Shine as a living star in praise of your Creator, and maintain the spirit of a saint.

❑ Attune yourself to oneness with the Infinite.

❑ Do your duties without cheating, and guard against being cheated.

❑ Correct from a calmer height of love and wisdom those who err by cheating, killing, and other vices of Satan.

❑ Think positively and constructively, and use the wisdom of all times to be a Master Builder.

Published Books

Management/Business

1. *Business Management and How to Achieve Organizational Goals*
2. *The Principles and Policies of Research Methodology*
3. *Contemporary Issues Which Determines the Dynamic Functions of Business Management*
4. *The Role of Ethics in Cooperate Governance*
5. *General Principles of Management and Research Methodology*

Philosophy

6. *Philosophy the Maker of Great Thinkers*
7. *The Fundamentals of Core Logic*
8. *The Twenty First Century Philosophical Caveats*

Religious/Inspirational

9. *Have You Discovered Your Assignment with Destiny?*
10. *A Great Personality Dwells in the Flesh*
11. *Wisdom is Wealth*
12. *Bring Out the Christ in You*
13. *Whose Vessel Are You?*
14. *What Makes Great Men*
15. *The Best Belongs to All*
16. *God's Gifts Are Irrevocable*
17. *Using Your Gifts to Help Others*

---

35. *Teach Yourself Research Techniques*
36. *The Evolving Dynamics of Business Strategy*
37. *The Dynamic Challenges of Organizational Growth*
38. *Business Strategy and Entrepreneurship Management*
39. *Understanding the Dynamics of Marketing Management*
40. *The Dynamic Role of Policy and Strategy in Economic Achievements*
41. *Strategy and Business Strategy*
42. *The Foundation of Natural Economics*
43. *Management and Motivation (Its Theory, Principles, and Practices)*
44. *The Benefits of Long Range Planning*
45. *Understanding the Effective Dynamics of Business Strategy*
46. *Effective Planning Key Factor to Business Success/Management*
47. *Computer Logic for Science and Engineering Students*
48. *The Imperatives of Computer Technology to Our Modern System Analysis*
49. *Creative Management with Computer Technology*

Philosophy

50. *The Importance of Logic and Diplomacy in Conflict Resolution*
51. *Plato's Philosophical Lamentation (Adept Series)*
52. *Akhenaten's Vision for Democracy and Philosophy (Adept Series)*
53. *Philosophy of Order of the Quest*
54. *The Power and Wisdom of the Unknown Philosopher (Columbus Readers/Adept Series)*
55. *Plato's Seven Point Discourses*
56. *Plato's Philosophical Constitution*
57. *Philosophy and Applied Logic*
58. *Introduction to the Anatomy of Transcendental Philosophy*
59. *The Dynamic Functions of Philosophy*
60. *The Scientific Application of Logic for the Benefit of the Internet Age*
61. *The Scientific Application of Logic to Quantum Physics*
62. *Philosophy and Logic for Modern Society*
63. *Philosophy, The Way of Great Thinkers*

133. *Philosophy and the Holy Bible*
134. *Philosophy and the Koran*
135. *The Objective Role of Philosophy and Reasoning*
136. *Philosophy and Evolution*
137. *The Immortality of Leonardo da Vinci*

Religious/Inspirational

138. *Abraham the Mystical Father of Faith*
139. *The Prodigal Pastor*
140. *The Inspired Life of Jesus (Adept Series)*
141. *Discovering the Fire of Christ in You*
142. *The Dangers of Spiritual Illiteracy*
143. *The Authority of Spiritual Powers*
144. *Divine Healing in a Contemporary Era*
145. *Another Book of the Proverbs*
146. *Spiritual Meditations Volumes 1 and 2*
147. *Affirmations to Solving Our Daily Problems*
148. *Man Is the Beauty of the Universe Volumes 1 and 2*
149. *Truth Is Universal Volumes 1 and 2*
150. *What Is Beyond God Volumes 1 and 2*
151. *The Value of a True Teacher*
152. *Man Who Do You Worship*
153. *The Purpose-Driven Workshop*
154. *The World Needs Servant*
155. *The Secrets of Divine Security*
156. *Divine Love Is Everything*
157. *The Secrets of Divine Security*
158. *Favour, Favours the Brave*
159. *When God Calls You a Saint*
160. *The Values and Virtues of Simplicity*
161. *The Values and Virtues of Illumined Parents*
162. *God Has Not Forgotten Man*
163. *Women Are the Aroma of Beauty*
164. *That Two May Be One*
165. *The Miraculous Power of Faith*
166. *The Unequalled Power of Love*
167. *Twelve Positive Guides for Achieving Success*

Wisdom Series

344. *The Life and Wisdom of Pure Souls*
345. *The World Has Many Eyes*
346. *Love Is the Supernatural Medicine of Honest Living*
347. *The Power of Wisdom of the Third Eye*
348. *The Wisdom of Cosmic Enlightenment*
349. *The Electric Nature of Wisdom*
350. *Mysticism and Wisdom in Practice*
351. *Wisdom the Supreme Knowledge of All Ages*
352. *How to Develop Your Genius with the Use and Application of Wisdom*
353. *The Bible and Wisdom*
354. *Wisdom and the Koran*
355. *Wisdom and Religion*
356. *Wisdom and Destiny in Manifestation*
357. *The Power of Wisdom in Ministration*
358. *How a Pastor Can Inspire His Knowledge with the Ingenious Wisdom of Inspiration*
359. *Man Is a Living Foundry of Inspiration*
360. *Creation Is a Comprehensive Revelation of the Power of Wisdom*
361. *Wisdom Is Spirit*
362. *Wisdom Is Consummate*
363. *The Unlimited Nature of Balanced Wisdom*
364. *Journey into Wisdom*
365. *Wisdom is Perfect Truth in Manifest*
366. *The Rhythm of Wisdom Is the Creative Pulsation of the Creator*
367. *A Mystic Is a Practional User of Ingenious*
368. *Wisdom in Service*
369. *Facts about the Wisdom of the Three Wise Men*
370. *The Wish of Wisdom*
371. *The Will of Wisdom*
372. *Living in the Supreme Light of Wisdom*
373. *The Mystical Wonders of the Cosmic Wisdom*
374. *Absolute Wisdom Is Only Acquired through the Balanced Knowledge of True Mysticism*

Metaphysics with Mysticism

Science and Technology

Health

672. The Mystical Values of Water
673. The Herbs and Roots Are Our Natural Physician
674. Nature Is Full of Medicine
675. The Mystical Wonders of the Plants
676. How to Use Natural Medicine to Make Orthodox Medicine More Effective
677. The Dynamism of Nature's Chemistry

Literature

678. The Price of Love
679. Man the Head of the Family
680. The Gentle Breeze
681. The Wicked Friend
682. The Endless Power of the Pen
683. The Oracle of Illiteracy
684. The Desert of Buds (Poem)
685. The Making of a Great Kingdom
686. The Evil Days of the Kings
687. Do Not Eat from the Cultist Table (Poetry)
688. Politics Is the Game of One with One Hand
689. Potters Possess Creative Wisdom (Poetry)
690. The Judges Cults Play Your Life with Love
691. Ekwubiri the Talkative
692. Alice Is a Divine Angel with the Wisdom of Angels Norms
693. Dangers of Deceitful Leadership
694. The Agony of a Leader
695. The Errors of Wrong Choice
696. The Regrets of a Cult Man with His Followers
697. How Do You Look at Your Wife
698. The Regrets of Political Adventure
699. Tell Me the Stories of Love
700. The Queen of Edo Kingdom Who Makes Her Hair in Benin Style
701. Kago Must Laugh
702. Abel the Bad Boy (The ABC of Literature)
703. Traveling with a Boat in the Desert
704. My Forests Friends

742. The Hairy Lady
743. The Faithful Servant
744. How to Win Your Spouse's Love
745. From the World Castle
746. My Wife Made Me to Remember My Mother
747. The Foolish Maid
748. The Pastor Who Employed Prostitute
749. The Sweetness of Sin
750. Politics Is a Game of Mediocre
751. The Odour of a Bad Teacher
752. The Character of a Bad Friend
753. Love Is Not Force
754. Mariam the Disobedient Daughter
755. Squirrels in Their Garden
756. The Story of My Pigeon
757. My Love for Nature
758. The Portrait of Love
759. How Eke Ate His Blood (The Story of a Painful Exit)

Adept Series

760. The Original Meaning of Kabala
761. The Wisdom of Kabala
762. The Reasoning for Kabala
763. Jesus and the Kabala
764. The Mystical Christ with the Key of Kabala
765. The Mystical Worship of the Kabala by the Gnostics
766. Gnostics and the Kabala
767. How Kabala Started the Growth of Mystical Knowledge
768. Every Gnostics Come from the Root of Kabala
769. Kabala Could Not Be Comprehended By the Uninformed Jews
770. True Mysticism Originated from the Practice of Kabala
771. Kabala and the Practice of Mystical Rituals
772. God the Light and Sound of Original Kabala
773. Kabala the Celestial Technology for the Immortal Ones
774. Kabala the Ministry of Pure Christian Mysticism
775. Kabala the Wisdom of Great Illumination

776. *Kabala the Origin of Alchemy*
777. *Kabala the Foundry of Mystical Engineering*
778. *Kabala the Faith of Real Mystics*
779. *Occult Kabala*
780. *Metaphysical Kabala*
781. *Grow with the Knowledge and Practice of Kabala and Go to Heaven*
782. *Christianity Does Not Know the Meaning and Language of Kabala*
783. *Kabala Is the Profound Teacher with Consummate Wisdom*
784. *When Will Man Start Thanking Kabala Steadily*
785. *Christ with the Infinite Trinity Started the Kabala*
786. *Life Is the Celebration of the Conquest of Kabala*
787. *Philosophy and Wisdom*
788. *What Is the Himalayas*
789. *The Agony of the Soul*
790. *The Grail Masters*
791. *The Order of the Gods*
792. *The Immortal Works of Paracelsus*
793. *Echoes from the Angels*
794. *The Mystery of the Serpent*
795. *The Physics of the Luna Eclipse*
796. *Praising the Unseen Powers*
797. *The Mystery of Celestial Light*
798. *The Wisdom of Celestial Life*
799. *The Perfect Soul*
800. *The Supreme Melody*
801. *The Aquarian Life of Our Cosmic Illuminates*
802. *Mysticism and the Hydrogen Age*
803. *Modern Trends in Knowledge and Wisdom*
804. *The Mystical Herbs*

Alchemical Series

805. *Alchemy and Engineering Creativity*
806. *Advancing the Course of Technology with the Use and Application of Core Alchemy*
807. *Nature Is the Foundry of Alchemy*

839. The Physics of Alchemy
840. Alchemy the Foundry of Modern Technology
841. Alchemy the Creative Engineering of the Oriental Wizards
842. Alchemy with Its Wholistic Transmutation of Technology
843. Alchemy the Divine Road Map to Investigative Technology Who Are the Forerunners of the Science of Alchemy
844. Alchemy and the New Millennium
845. Give Me Alchemy and I Will Give You Creative Invention
846. Alchemy and the Jet Age
847. How Alchemy Was Used to Advance the Computer Age with Its Technology
848. Alchemy the Foundry of Polymer Androbotic Science and Engineering
849. Cosmic Alchemy
850. Cosmic Union
851. Meta-Cosmic Vision
852. Engineering and Transmutation

Grace Series

853. Are You in the List of Divine Grace
854. Is Your Grace Anointed?
855. His Grace Is Sufficient
856. His Grace Is Love Eternal
857. His Grace Is Driven with Light
858. Pray for the Love of the Grace
859. All Life Is Fathomed by the Grace
860. His Grace Is Our Shelter
861. Christ Is the Pinnacle of His Grace
862. His Grace Works Wonders
863. The Miracle of Supreme Grace
864. When Grace Is at Work
865. The Power of Working Grace
866. The Wisdom of Living Grace
867. Creation Is the Power of Grace
868. Empower Your Life with Grace
869. Wisdom Is the Product of Grace
870. Strive to Know What Lied Ahead of Your Grace

871. Your Destiny Is the Product of Divine Grace
872. Grace Made Abraham to Have Faith in God
873. Grace Is God in Action
874. Grace Is God in Glory
875. Life Is Best Lived with Grace
876. Every Prayer Must Be Said with the Wisdom of Grace
877. When Grace Speaks the Heavens Are Positively Provoked
878. Grace Makes One to Live a Purpose-Driven Life
879. The Living Church Is Founded on the Power and Wisdom of Grace
880. We Must Ask with Grace
881. Every Family Must Dwell on the Absolute Power of Grace
882. Grace Empowered Christ to Be Victorious
883. The Products of Grace Are Success and Victory
884. Grace Cannot Be a Victim
885. Strive to Make Grace Your Portion
886. No Problem of Life Is Mightier than the Power of Grace
887. Grace Is Life and Light
888. Life Lived without Grace Is Vanity upon Vanity
889. Man Has Not Known the Power of Grace
890. Only Grace Speaks about the Wonders and Wisdom of God
891. To Live with Grace Is to Live with the Best
892. When We Ask in Grace, We Must Receive in Grace
893. Inventions and Science Are the Products and Wonders of Grace
894. Divine Love Is Only Guaranteed by Blissful Grace
895. Grace Is the Nature of God
896. Peace and Unity Is the Product of Grace
897. Marriage Is a Divine Symbol of Grace
898. Grace Empowered Knowledge to Be the Beacon of True Living
899. Grace Is the Greatest Teacher of All Ages
900. Grace Is a Divine Current
901. Every Prayer Must Be Centred and Driven with the Power of Grace
902. Grace Authored the First Man
903. Light Is the Product of Grace
904. Every Genius Functions with Immeasurable Grace

905. The Life of the World Is Life in Manifest
906. Nothing in Life Can Quantify the Power of Grace
907. Grace Wrote the Bible and Other Immortal Works
908. Grace Brought Salvation to the World
909. The Worth of Grace Cannot Be Measured
910. Grace Is a Consummate Giver
911. Grace Is a Peculiar Lover
912. Grace Is a Physician
913. The Power of Grace Is Universal
914. The Spiritual Importance of Grace Is Revealed in the Prayer Which Reads Thus: May the Grace of Our Lord Jesus Christ, the Love of God and the Still Fellowship of Our Lord Jesus Christ, Be with Us Now and Forevermore

Drama

915. What Happens when the Pope Hears What?
916. My Wife's Pregnancy Is Not from Me

Women Series

917. The Lady of Knowledge
918. The Wisdom of an Experienced and Virtuous Mother
919. The Lady of Love
920. The Lady of Light
921. The Lady of Wealth
922. The Women of Vision
923. The Sweet Memories of My Mother
924. The Similarities of My Wife and My Mother
925. The Man Is the Beauty of the Wife
926. The Wife Is the Strength of the Husband
927. My Wife Is My Password
928. Marriage Is a Divine Testimony with Assorted Experience
929. Women and Nature's Medicine
930. Women Are Psychically Gifted
931. Women Are Natural Angels
932. Where Are the African Angels

Mathematical Series

933. *The Anatomy of Mathematics*
934. *Evolutionary Mathematics*
935. *The Dynamism of Mathematical Reasoning*
936. *Pythagoras and the Doctrine of Mathematics*
937. *Mathematical Symbolism*
938. *Mathematical Logic*
939. *Mathematical Key Words*
940. *Metaphysics and Mathematics*
941. *Diplomacy and Mathematics*
942. *Modern Mathematics with Economics*
943. *Modern Engineering Mathematics*
944. *Analytical Mathematics*
945. *Mathematics and Data Processing*
946. *Modern Mathematics with the Reasoning of Technology*
947. *Informative Mathematics*
948. *Logic Mathematics*
949. *The Dynamic Functions of General Mathematics*
950. *Creative Mathematics for Technologists*
951. *Wisdom and Mathematics Action*
952. *The History of Mathematics*
953. *Mathematical Mechanics*
954. *Understanding the Metalogic Principles of Mathematics*
955. *Seminar Papers Ranging from Philosophy, Science/ Technology, Economy to Governments Etc.*

Time Series

956. *The Immortality Wisdom of Time*
957. *There Is Time for Everything*
958. *The Gnostical Wisdom of Time (Adept Series)*
959. *The Wisdom and Wonders of Time*
960. *Nature Is the Mother of Time*
961. *There Is No Time in Space*
962. *Time Is a Factor of Creation*
963. *Man Fails Time*
964. *The Glory and Greatness of Time*

1000. The Aquarian Gospel of Time
1001. Develop and Increase Your Courage with Time
1002. The Aquarian Gospel of Time (Time Series)
1003. How Will I Be Received by the Angels at the Time of My Home Call
1004. The Mysteries of Eternal Time (Adept Series)
1005. He Does Not Fail in His Time
1006. The Moonlight Time and Other Events

Nature Series

1007. The Creative Power of Nature
1008. Nature Is Gentle, Long, Kind and Peaceful
1009. The Dynamic Wisdom of Nature
1010. Nature Is the Supreme Fulcrum of the Universe
1011. Nature Tells the Story of Birth and Rebirth in a Plain Language
1012. The Marvelous Wonders of Nature
1013. Nature Is a Perfect Physician
1014. Heal Yourself through the Power of Nature
1015. Inspiration Is the Monumental Language of Nature
1016. Nature Creates with Balance
1017. Balanced Interchange Is the Law of Nature
1018. Nature Is Homogeneity in Action
1019. Try to Think along with Nature
1020. A Talk to Nature Is a Talk to All Things
1021. I Appreciate Nature for Its Illumined Wisdom
1022. Learn to Work Knowingly with Nature (Adept Series)
1023. All Great Immortals Listened to Nature
1024. Nature's Heartbeat Is Mystical (Adept Series)
1025. The Cosmic Wonders of Nature (Adept Series)
1026. Nature Is a Symbol of Supreme Intelligence
1027. Have You Recognized Your Assignment with Mother Nature
1028. Nature Reveals Great Arts to Man
1029. Man Has Not Known His Natural Essence
1030. Nature Is a Great Teacher
1031. Nature Reasons with the Creator
1032. The Love of Nature Is a Supreme Gift

1033. *Man Is a Consummate Anatomy of Nature*
1034. *The Nature of the Stars Are Mystical Mystery*
1035. *All the Planets Love and Respect Nature*
1036. *The Creative Nature of the Universe Is a Perfect Aesthetism*
1037. *My Simple Garden Tells How Beautiful and Wonderful Nature Is*
1038. *Our Flowers Reveal the Greatness of Nature*
1039. *Nature Is a Great Historian*
1040. *Nature Is a Living Philosophy*
1041. *The Science of Nature Is Written on a Simple Marble*
1042. *Learn How to Respect Nature and in Turn It Will Love You with Perfect Protection*
1043. *The Man Who Talks with the Flowers Appreciates the Value of Nature*
1044. *An Angry Man Does Not Reason with Nature*
1045. *A Meditation Which Nature Is a Direct Communion with the Blessed*
1046. *Angels Speak about Nature with a Great Homily*
1047. *Christ Worked with Nature Which Informed Him to Become the Supreme Master of the Universe (Adept Series)*
1048. *The Universe Is Authored along with Nature's Rhythm*
1049. *Simply Tells Nature the Truth*
1050. *Nature Reads Man More than Man Knows Nature*
1051. *Nature Is a Provisional Encyclopedia*
1052. *There Is a Supreme Partnership between Nature and Wisdom*
1053. *The Fire of Inspiration Is an Eternal Motion (Adept Series)*
1054. *Give Nature a Chance to Perform and It Will Surely Dazzle You with Wonders*
1055. *Man-Woman Electrifying Balance Is Naturally a Monumental Interchange*
1056. *No Human Being Is Capable of Changing Nature and This is Why Science Cannot Charge Nor Recharge Nature*
1057. *Nature Is a Consummate Mathematician*
1058. *Nature Started the Act of Creation and This is Why the History of Birth and Rebirth Speak Volumes about Nature*
1059. *A Praise to the Wonders of Nature Is a Glorious Praise to the Consummate Creator of All Ages*
1060. *When You Are Tired Allow Nature to Recharge You*

1061. Nature Is a Mystical Physician Whose Charges Are Naturally Free

1062. How Sweet Is the Reality of Nature and How Wonderful Will Man Be When He Works along with Nature

1063. Man Is a Monumental Marble of Mother Nature

1064. All Works Which Does Not Invite Nature into It Is as Vantiy as the Concept

1065. A Lion Is Always Asking Nature to Protect Her

1066. Nature Is the Brain Box of All Compositive Creativity

1067. The Supreme Messenger of Light Came from the Abundant Bank of Divine Nature

1068. All Great Men Live in Nature's Garden

1069. No Man Can Comprehend nor Quantify the Wisdom of Nature

1070. Nature Sings All the Time with Adoration and Perfect Melodies to the Origin of Its Greatness

1071. Mozart the Supreme Master of Water Music Was First Possessed by the Wisdom and Supremacy of Mother Nature

1072. Nature Tells Us How Beautiful Our Echoes Are

1073. A Look at the Top Mountains Reveals How Powerful, Wonderful, Monumental and Mysterious Nature Is

1074. A Look at the Beach Tells Man That Nature Is Aesthetically Milicential

1075. The Man Who Understands Nature Appreciates the Value of Creation

1076. The Creator Appeared First to Man at the Garden of Genesis

1077. Physical Death at Any Point in Time Tells Us the Value of Nature through the Process of Composition and Decomposition

1078. Any Man Who Puts Nature into Action Must Certainly Get to the Mountain Peak without Disturbance

1079. Nature Directed the Three Wise Men to Locate Bethlehem

1080. Technology Reveals the Greatness of Nature's Aesthetism

1081. Engineering at Any Point in Time Is Always Adopting Nature as a Consummate Consultant

1112. **Most Geniuses Are Musicians**
1113. **The Story of Kant Village Is Narrated in Music**
1114. **Solomon Wrote the Songs of Songs and the Songs of Sorrows with Music**
1115. **The Mystical Powers of Music Made Paul and Silas to Become Friends to the Lions**
1116. **The Man Who Authored the First Music Showed Men the Way to Heaven**
1117. **Heaven Is a Celebration of Celestial Melodies**
1118. **The Power of Praises Brought Me Closer to My Creator**
1119. **Use the Power of Music to Will Your Way Through**
1120. **Music Makes You to Rubbish Challenges**
1121. **Great Amnesty Goes with Songs and Melodies**
1122. **The Man Who Wrote the Sacred Songs and Solos Is a Mystic**

Faith Series

1123. **Faith Is Real**
1124. **Faith Is Life**
1125. **Faith Is Purposeful and Powerful**
1126. **Faith is Courageous**
1127. **Faith Is Wisdom in Divine Manifestation**
1128. **Living Faith Brings Man Closer to His Creator**
1129. **Abraham Is Faithful to God**
1130. **Faith Must Function with Work**
1131. **All Great Souls Lived for Faith**
1132. **Jesus Is the Supreme Victory of Faith**
1133. **You Must Put Your Faith into Work**
1134. **Victory Is the Product of Faith**
1135. **You Must Have a Living Garden of Faith**
1136. **All Faithful Men Are Spiritually Tireless**
1137. **Jesus Built the Church on Faith**
1138. **The Mission of Calvary Was Destroyed with the Power of Faith**
1139. **Great Works Are Written on the Victory and Vision of Faith**
1140. **Man Where Is Thy Faith**
1141. **I Treasure the Ordination of Faith**
1142. **A Blessed Man Is a Victor of Faith**

Marriage Series

1203. *Mothers Are Millicents to Marriage (MMM)*

Agricultural Series

1204. *Agricultural Engineering in Our Contemporary Era*
1205. *The Economic Importance of Agriculture*
1206. *The Importance of Fishery in Economic Development*
1207. *Problems Facing Agriculture in Our Contemporary Era*
1208. *The Importance of Soil Conservation*
1209. *Pest Control and Agricultural Development in Third World Countries*
1210. *The Importance of Research and Development in the Agricultural Sector*
1211. *Understanding the Dynamics of Forest Preservation*
1212. *The Economic Importance of Agricultural Products*
1213. *Utilizing the Goldmine of Agricultural Technology to Enhance the Goldmines of Our Economy*
1214. *Understanding the Economic Importance of Crop Research*
1215. *The Importance of Climatic Change to Agricultural Development*
1216. *Improving the Standard of Our National Economy with the Use and Application of Agricultural Technology*
1217. *Providing Employment Opportunities with the Use and Application of Agricultural Development*
1218. *General Agricultural Science for Higher Institutions*
1219. *The Importance of Plant Technology in Agricultural Development*
1220. *General Agricultural Science for Higher Institutions*
1221. *The Economic Importance of Bee Farming*
1222. *Problems Facing Agricultural Development in Our Contemporary Era*

Thought Series

1223. *Only in Positive Thinking Lies the Secrets of Creation*
1224. *Where Are the Thinking Men of Africa*
1225. *God Is the Only Consummate Thinker*
1226. *Learn How to Think Inwardly*